Recipes of Canadian Martyrs and St. Margaret Mary Church

The Recipes of the Canadian Martyrs and St. Margaret Mary's Churches

by

Frank Hegyi with Contributors of Recipes

Recipes of Canadian Martyrs and St. Margaret Mary Church

Published by

Frank Hegyi Publications Ottawa, Ontario, Canada
www.fhegyi.com

@ Frank Hegyi 2021

ISBN 978-0-9940201-5-4

frank@fhegyi.com

All rights reserved

Recipes of Canadian Martyrs and St. Margaret Mary Church

Contents

Acknowledgment 13

Appetizers 15

    Spicy Chicken Wings 16

    Caramel Apple Cream Cheese Spread 17

    Bread and kielbasa 18

    Antipasto Loaf 19

    Swedish Butter Balls 20

    Maids of Honour 21

    Onion Cheese Dip 22

    Apple Crisp 23

    Cranberry Feta Pinwheels 24

    White Wine Sangria 25

    Mozzarella Sticks 26

    Homemade Lemonade 27

    Zucchini Relish 28

    Mediterranean Cheese Marinade 29

    Pesto Appetizer 30

Breakfast 31

    Omelette Indian Style 32

    Hungarian omelette 33

    Ham and Eggs 34

    Potato pancakes 35

    Turkish Poached Eggs 36

    Easy flavour packed Lemonade 37

Cranberry Pancakes 39
Soups 41
Gulyas Soup (Gulyás leves) 42
Borsc (Ukrainian) 43
Black Bean Soup 44
Thai Shrimp Soup 45
Butter Nut Squash Soup 46
Roasted Red Pepper Soup 47
Chicken/Turkey and Red Lentil Soup 48
Mushroom Pancetta Soup 49
Creamy Carrot Coconut soup 50
Garlic Soup 51
Pea Soup 52
Cold Cranberry Soup 53
Cabbage Soup 54
Chicken Broth "pour le rhume" 55
Polish Mushroom Soup 56
Minestrone soup 57
Cioppino Soup 58
Golden Carrot Soup 59
Dill Pickle (Ogorki) Soup 60
Dutch Pea Soup 61
Old Fashioned Pea Soup 62
Poultry 63
Hungarian chicken paprikás 64

Hungarian Wienerschnitze 65

Turkey, Spinach and Pasta 66

Best Ever Chicken Pate 67

Chicken with mushrooms 68

Tomato Slow Cooker Chicken 69

Chicken Thighs 70

Amaretto Chicken 71

Spinach and Beet Salad with Chicken 72

Cashew Chicken 73

Breaded and Baked Chicken 74

Chicken and Wild Rice Casserole 75

Lemon Glazed Chicken 76

Coq au Vin 77

Fried Chicken 78

Meat 79

Hungarian Goulash (Pörkölt) 80

Schnitzel Pork Cutlets 81

BBQ steak and potatoes 82

BBQ Ribs in the Crock Pot 83

Blue Cheese Crusted Filet Mignon 84

Toad in the Hole 85

Marla's Maple Pork 86

Bacon Wrapped Pork Loin 87

Homemade Kebab and Salad 88

Souvlaki 90

Lillian's Meat Balls ... 91
Beef Hot Pot ... 92
Quiche Lorraine ... 93
Norma's Sparerib ... 94
Beef Tourtiere ... 95
Moroccan Chicken Stew ... 96
Ryan's Favorite beef ... 97

Fish ... 99
Fisherman's delight (halaszle) ... 100
Baked Salmon ... 101
Mustard salmon ... 102
Quick Shrimp and Corn Chowder ... 103
Sweet Potato Chili Casserole ... 104
Low Carb Sausage ... 105
Mussels Provençale ... 106
Baked Fish ... 109
Tuna Twirl Surprise ... 110
Crab Foo Yung ... 111
Shrimp Basil ... 112
Tuna Macaroni Casserole ... 113
Salmon Quiche ... 114

Vegetarian and Pasta ... 115
Cabbage Rolls Holubtsi ... 116
Vegetarian Lecsó ... 117
Hungarian Nokedli ... 118

Noodles and rice with peas	119
Spaghetti Carbonara	120
Horseradish Smashed Potatoes	121
Oma Trudi's Dough Andress Dumplings	122
Individual Plum Tarts	124
Bud Hendley's Spaghetti Sauce	126
Ben's Lasagna	127
Brussels Sprouts	129
Crepes	130
Scalloped Potatoes	131
Baked Pasta Florentine	132
Cheese Shells	133
Greek Pasta Salad	134
Yummy carrot cake with cream cheese icing	135
Chicken Curry with Red Peppers	137
Penne, Prosciutto and Peas	138
Fresh Pasta	139
Banana Breads	140
Bachelor Buttons	141
Summer Pasta	142
Ginger cookies	143
Cheesecake Cupcakes	144
Never Fail Flakey Pie Crust	145
No-longer Vegan Fettuccine	146
Lemon Zucchini Bread	147

Pumpkin bread 149
Vegetarian Casserole 150
Rice Casserole 151
Gujerati Style Green Beans 152
Scallop Potatoes with Rosemary 153
Vegetable Lasagna 154
Hash Brown Potato Casserole 155
African Winter Vegetable Stew 156
Zucchini-Cheese Casserole 157
Instructions 157
Penne with Artichokes and Feta 159
Potato and Carrot Casserole 161
Scalloped Potatoes 162
Spinach and Cheese Casserole 164
Vegetable Side Dish 165
Salads 167
Hungarian Cucumber salad 168
Pomegranite and Feta Salad 169
BLT Chopped Salad 170
Mango Salad 171
No Bake Key Lime Pie in a Jar 172
Broccoli Salad 173
Grilled Zucchini & Buffalo Mozzarella Salad 174
"Salade d'amour" 175
Mexican Salad Bowl 176

Spicy Chili 177

Garden-fresh Corn Salad 178

Holiday Salad 179

Quinoa Salad with Peaches 180

Cold Chicken Salad 181

24 Hour Salad 182

Orange Pecan Salad 183

Curried Lentil salad 184

Orange Poppy Seed Salad 185

Chinese Salad 186

Thai Pear Salad 187

Bean Salad 188

Cranberry Pear Relish 189

Herb-Glazed Brussels Sprouts 190

Green Bean and Walnut Salad 191

Byward Maple Parsnips 192

Blue Cheese Salad Dressng 193

Thai Grilled Beef Salad 194

Dips and Spread 195

Satay Pork with Peanut Sauce 196

Chicken or pork, cut into cubes 197

Crabmeat Spread 198

Fried Noodles 199

Tabouli 200

Asparagus Dip 201

Pineapple Cream Fruit Dip 202
Herbed Vegetable Dip 203
Salsa 204
Hot Crab Dip 205
Hot Crab Dip 205
Desserts 207
Hungarian Palacsinta 208
English trifle 209
Shortbread Cookies 210
Lebanese knafeh jibneh 211
Sour cream Rhubarb Crisp 213
Caramelized Apple Puree 214
Katie Coonen's Oreo Ice Cream Torte 215
Delicious Coffee Cake 216
Walnut Romesco 217
Tea Biscuits 218
Maple pie 219
Dog Biscuits 220
Chocolate Cherry Balls 221
Overnight Buns 222
Lazy Gourmet Carrot Cake 223
Easy Sugar Cookies 224
Chocolate Chip Cake 225
Easy Chocolate Cake 226
Potato Scones 227

Best chocolate zucchini brownies	228
Crème Brule Cheesecake	230
Chocolate Mounds	231
Cheesecake Cupcakes	232
Whitewater Granola Bars	233
Grandma Grady's Apple Pie	234
Cinnamon Swirl Apple Bread	236
Apple Cake Tartin - Ina Garten	238
Hot Fudge Pudding	240
Blueberry Kuchen	241
Boule de Neige	242
Banana Bread	243
Flourless Chocolate Cake	244
Poor Boy Cake	245
Aunt Julia's Torte	246
Plum (or other fruit) Custard "Pie"	247
Happiness Cake	249
Blueberry Muffins	250
Almond Biscotti	251
Double Chocolate Brownies	252
Oatmeal Lace Cookies	253
Peanut Butter Marshmallow Treats	254
Almond Butter Crunch	255
Chocolate Chip Cake	256
Hazelnut Vanilla Shortbread	257

Recipes of Canadian Martyrs and St. Margaret Mary Church

Rum Cake 258
Brandy Sauce 259
Chocolate Peanut Butter Balls 260
Cranberry Bread 261
Fiesta Cheese Dip Cake 262
Chocolate Peanut Butter Cake 263
Moist Shortcake 264
Julie's fluffy Frosting 265
Rhubarb Meringue Pie 266
Sugar Pie 267
Turtles 268
Cherry Almond Nanaimo Bars 269
Cheese Pie 270
Peanut Butter Bars 271
Baked Apple Delight 272
Rhubarb-Orange Coffee Cake 273

Recipes of Canadian Martyrs and St. Margaret Mary Church

Acknowledgment

The contributors wish to thank the users to have a successful cooking experience. The pictures included with the recipes are from internet and may show some variations from the actual recipes.

A special thank you are also due to Father Tim Coonen, who was involved in editing the manuscript.

Abbreviations

tsp = teaspoon

tbsp. = tablespoon

lb(s) = pound(s)

g = gram(s)

oz = ounce(s)

pkg = package

Recipes of Canadian Martyrs and St. Margaret Mary Church

Recipes of Canadian Martyrs and St. Margaret Mary Church

Appetizers

Frank Hegyi

Fr. Tim Coonen

Maureen Cerroni

Recipes of Canadian Martyrs and St. Margaret Mary Church
Spicy Chicken Wings   Frank Hegyi

Ingredients

1 can (8 oz.) tomato sauce
5 tsp red pepper flakes
2 tbsp. hot sauce
1 tbsp garlic powder

3 tsp onion powder
2 jalapeno peppers, chopped
1 lb chicken wings
3 tsp paprika

Spicy chicken wings[1]

Instructions

1. Combine tomato sauce, red pepper flakes, hot sauce, garlic powder, onion powder, paprika and Jalapeno peppers in a medium size bowl.
2. Spray a baking sheet with no-stick cooking spray.
3. Place chicken wings on baking sheet
4. Brush the sauce over wings.
5. Bake at 350 F for 20 minutes. Turnover and brush with sauce and bake for another 10 minutes.

---

[1] https://www.readyseteat.com/advanced-search?keywords=chicken+wings

Recipes of Canadian Martyrs and St. Margaret Mary Church

Caramel Apple Cream Cheese Spread

Pamela DiNardo

Ingredients

8 oz of cream cheese   4 tbsp toffee bits (skors)
½ cup caramel sauce   4 apples or pears, cored and thinly sliced

Caramel Apple Cream Cheese Spread[2]

Instructions

1. Place the block of cream cheese on a serving plate.
2. Use the back of a spoon to create a small well in the top of the cream cheese.
3. Spoon the caramel sauce into the well, allowing some to drip over the sides. Sprinkle with toffee bits.
4. Serve with sliced apple and pear

---

[2] http://www.kraftrecipes.com/recipes/caramel-apple-dip-53060.aspx

Recipes of Canadian Martyrs and St. Margaret Mary Church
Bread and kielbasa   Frank Hegyi

Ingredients

1 baguette   300 g lean Kielbasa
100 g butter   3 tsp paprika

Kielbasa[3]

Instructions

1. Cut Kielbasa into thinly slides and place them on a cookie sheet, then on a BBQ.
2. Cut baguette into 1 inch slices.
3. Spread each baguette with butter and sprinkle on paprika.
4. Serve on a platter.

---

[3] 3 http://allrecipes.com/recipe/219021/spaetzle-sauerkraut-and-sausage-casserole/?internalSource=recipe

Antipasto Loaf — Pamela DiNardo

Ingredients

1 French bread baguette
1 tub (8 oz) Cream cheese spread
½ cup drained marinated artichoke hearts, chopped
2 cups baby spinach leaves, chopped
½ cup drained oil packed sun dried tomatoes, chopped
3 tbsp pesto
2 tbsp grated parmesan cheese

Antipasto Loaf[4]

Instructions

1. Cut baguette lengthwise in half.
2. Remove soft insides from both bread halves, reserve to make bread crumbs or croutons
3. Mix cream cheese spread and pesto; spread evenly onto insides of bread shells.
4. Fill evenly with tomatoes, artichokes, Parmesan cheese and spinach
5. Reassemble baguette; wrap tightly in plastic wrap.
6. Refrigerate at least 1 hour or overnight.
7. Slice 1- inch thick and arrange on platter to serve.

---

[4] http://www.kraftrecipes.com/recipes/antipasto-loaf-106401.aspx

Recipes of Canadian Martyrs and St. Margaret Mary Church

Swedish Butter Balls   Pamela DiNardo

Ingredients

1 cup butter softened   ½ cup sifted icing sugar
1 tsp vanilla   2 ½ cups flour
1 cup chopped pecans   Icing Sugar

Swedish butter balls[5]

Instructions

1. Cream butter, icing sugar and vanilla together.
2. Add flour and mix well.
3. Stir in nuts
4. Shape dough into 1" balls. Place on ungreased cookie sheet.
5. Bake at 400 for 8-12 minutes. Cool on racks, roll in sifted icing sugar. Makes 4 dozen.

---

[5] http://www.cdkitchen.com/recipes/recs/574/Swedish-Butter-Balls83041.shtml

Recipes of Canadian Martyrs and St. Margaret Mary Church

Maids of Honour   Pamela DiNardo

Ingredients

2 cup flour
1 tbsp white sugar
¼ cup butter
¼ cup milk
2 tbsp butter, softened
2 tbsp fruit preserves

1 tbsp all-purpose flour
¼ tsp nutmeg
2 eggs beaten
2 tbsp cream sherry
¾ ground almonds
¾ cup white sugar

Maids of Honour

Instructions

1. In medium bowl, stir together 1 cup flour and 1 tablespoon sugar. Cut in ¼ cup butter until smaller than peas. Sprinkle 1 tablespoon of milk at a time over the dough until moistened.
2. Cut into 2 ½ inch circles using a cookie or biscuit cutter. Press circles into the bottom and up the sides of ungreased mini muffin cups, set aside.
3. In a medium bowl, cream together 2 tablespoons butter, ¾ cup sugar and 1 tablespoon flour. Beat in the eggs and sherry, then stir in the ground almonds.
4. Place ¼ teaspoon of jam into the bottom of the lined cups. Cover with 1 tablespoon of the almond mixture.
5. Bake for 15 – 20 minutes in the preheated oven, until the tops are lightly browned. Allow to cool slightly before removing from muffin tins to cool on wire racks.

---

[6] http://allrecipes.com/recipe/26166/maids-of-honor/

Recipes of Canadian Martyrs and St. Margaret Mary Church
Onion Cheese Dip   Pamela DiNardo

Ingredients

1 cup grated Emmental Cheese
1 cup Hellman's Mayonnaise (never use Miracle Whip, it won't work)
1 cup chopped or very thinly sliced onion (preferably vidalia)
Mix all three together

Onion Cheese Dip[7]

Instructions

1. Put on 1or 2 shallow baking dishes
2. Cook in 325-degree oven for 20 minutes until hot and slightly browned at top edges
3. Serve with French bread, pita triangles, corn chips or what ever else.

---

[7] http://www.kraftcanadcom/recipes/double-onion-dip-90266?cm_mmc=srch-g-_-Kraft-Dips-Onion-EN-_-onion-dip

Recipes of Canadian Martyrs and St. Margaret Mary Church

Apple Crisp   Pamela DiNardo

Ingredients

Preheat oven to 350 F   1 cup of rolled oats
1 cup flour   1 tsp of cinnamon
1 cup light brown sugar   ½ cup of butter or margarine
2 cups sliced apples
Mix together until it resembles fine crumbs, set aside

Apple Crisp[8]

Instructions

1. Peel, core and slice apples, place in casserole dish, sprinkle mixture on top and bake for approximately 20 minutes or until apples are soft
2. Depending on apples, I sometimes add a little water to the pan to help soften up the apples. Nobody likes a hard apple crisp!!

---

[8]http://www.kraftcanada.com/search?searchTerm=apple+crisp&cm_mmc=srch-_-YaBing-_-Kraft-Baking-Apple-Crisp-EN-_-apple-crisp

Cranberry Feta Pinwheels   Pamela DiNardo

Ingredients

1 carton whipped cream cheese
1 cup crumbled Feta Cheese
4 flour tortila
1 pkg dried cranberries
¼ cup chopped onions

Cranberry Feta Pinwheels[9]

Instructions

1. Combine cream cheese, feta cheese and onions.
2. Stir in cranberries, spread over tortilla, roll tightly and refrigerate at least one hour.
3. Cut each tortilla into 10 slices.

---

[9] https://www.tasteofhome.com/recipes/cranberry-feta-pinwheels

White Wine Sangria — Pamela DiNardo

Ingredients

1 bottle dry white wine
2 tbsp super fine sugar
2 tbsp Calvados
1 bottle Perrier
2 kiwi fruit, sliced
1 cup seedless green grapes
2 tbsp Cointreau
1 large pear, cored and sliced, red pear is nice contrast in colours

White Wine Sangria[10]

Instructions

1. Pour wine into a large, preferable glass pitcher.
2. Add sugar and stir to dissolve thoroughly.
3. Add liqueurs and stir again.
4. Add fruits, cover and refrigerate for 4-5 hours
5. When ready to serve, stir well, add Perrier and pour over ice in white wine glass.

---

[10] http://allrecipes.com/recipes/242/drinks/sangria/

Recipes of Canadian Martyrs and St. Margaret Mary Church

Mozzarella Sticks
Pamela DiNardo

Ingredients

12 pieces string cheese
12 egg roll wrappers

Oil for deep fat frying
Marinara or spaghetti sauce

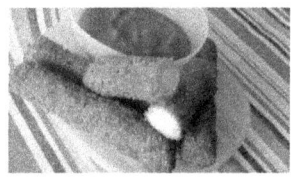

Mozzarella Sticks[11]

Instructions

1. Place a piece of string cheese near the bottom corner of one of the egg roll wrapper (keep remaining wrappers covered with a damp paper towel until ready to use)
2. Fold bottom corner over cheese.
3. Roll up halfway; fold sides toward center over cheese.
4. Moisten remaining corner with water; roll up tightly to seal. Repeat with remaining wrappers and cheese.
5. In a frying pan, heat ½ inch of oil, fry sticks a few at a time for 30 – 60 seconds on each side until golden brown.
6. Drain on paper towels. Serve with Marinara Sauce

---

[11] http://allrecipes.com/recipe/214159/homemade-mozzarella-stick

Homemade Lemonade — Kelly Langill

Ingredients

1 1/4 cups sugar
1 cup water
1 cup lemon juice

Homemade Lemonade[12]

Instructions

1. Add sugar to water and bring to a boil. When the sugar is dissolved (almost immediately), remove from heat and let cool.
2. When cool add the lemon juice. This is the concentrate.
3. To serve, add 1/3 concentrate and 2/3 water (or soda water) to a pitcher.
4. You can dress up the pitcher by adding mint leaves and fresh cut lemon slices.

---

[12] http://www.simplyrecipes.com/recipes/perfect_lemonade/

Recipes of Canadian Martyrs and St. Margaret Mary Church

Zucchini Relish
Cathy Clifford

Ingredients

3 lbs zucchini squash (+/- 10 medium- sized)   3 onions
2 red peppers
Shred vegetables in food processor. Add 1/4 cup pickling salt. Let stand 1 hour. Drain off excess liquid.
Add the following ingredients to the vegetable mix and bring to boil in large pot.

2 1/2 cups sugar   1 1/2 cups white vinegar
1 1/2 tsp dry mustard   1 tsp celery seeds
1 tsp black pepper   1/2 tsp tumeric

Zucchini Relish[13]

Instruction

1. Thicken with Solution of 1 tbsp water and 2 tbsp cornstarch.
2. Transfer to sterilized jars for canning.

---

[13]htts://www.bing.com/search?q=zucchini+relish&form=PRDLCS&pc=MDDCJS&httpsmsn

Recipes of Canadian Martyrs and St. Margaret Mary Church

Mediterranean Cheese Marinade   Barb Popel

Ingredients

½ cup black olives
3 tbsp parsley leaves
¼ cup fresh basil,
¼- ½ tbsp black peppercorns
2 cloves garlic
1 lb. goat cheese, cut into 3 or 4 slices

¼ cup sun dried tomatoes
2 sprigs fresh rosemary
1 tbsp fresh thyme
a few red chili flakes
1 cup extra virgin olive oil

Mediterranean Cheese Marinade[14]

Instructions

1. Cut goat cheese into 4 slices and lay the goat cheese flat in a pan.
2. Mix marinade of sliced black olives, chopped sun dried tomatoes, chopped parsley leaves, rosemary, chopped basil, thyme, cracked black peppercorn, chilli flakes, pressed garlic and olive oil. Pour marinade over goat cheese.
3. Let stand, covered, at room temperature for at least 6 hours before serving. Drain off and save most of the marinade prior to serving. Serve on sliced baguettes.

---

[14]https://www.bing.com/search?q=Mediterranean+Cottage+Cheese+Dip&filters=ufn%3a%22Mediterranean+Cottage+Cheese+Dip

Recipes of Canadian Martyrs and St. Margaret Mary Church

Pesto Appetizer　　　　　　　　　　　　Barbara Fischer

Ingredients

Green pesto　　　　　　　　　　Pita bread
Cheddar cheese　　　　　　　　Feta cheese
Sundried tomatoes

Pesto Appetizer[15]

Instructions

1. Spread peso on pita bread.
2. Top with cheese and diced, sun dried tomato.
3. Bake in oven until cheese is melted.
4. Cut into wedges when cool.
5. You may add any topping, just like a pizza. Vegetarian items seem to work best.

---

[15] https://www.bing.com/search?q=Tomato-Pesto+Appetizers&filters=ufn%3a%22Tomato-Pesto+

Breakfast

Dianne Borg

Pamela DiNardo

Nancy MacDonald

Omelette Indian Style — Frank Hegyi

Ingredients

6 eggs beaten into a mixture
1 onion, chopped in small cubes
2 green chillies finely chopped
¼ cup vegetable oil
1 tsp coriander leaves

1 tsp salt
1 tsp Pepper
1 tsp dill
1 tsp fresh ginger root
1 tsp fresh garlic

Omelette Indian Style[16]

Instruction

1. Place onions, chillies, pepper, dill, ginger (chopped up), garlic and coriander (chopped up) in a large bowl and mix.
2. Place eggs in a separate bowl, mix, and add onion mixture and salt and place it in a large pan.
3. Finish cooking.

---

[16] http://blogexplore.com/food/breakfast/masala-omelette-indian-style-omelette- recipe/

Hungarian omelette — Frank Hegyi

Ingredients

6 eggs beaten into a mixture
1 onion, chopped
1 green pepper chopped
1 tsp cayenne
½ cup vegetable oil

1 tsp salt
1 tsp black pepper
1 tsp dill
1 red pepper

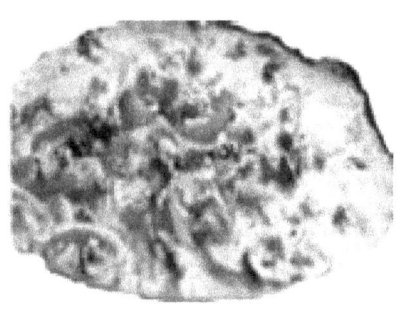

Hungarian Omelette[17]

Instructions

1. Place onions, green pepper, red pepper, dill, and cayenne in a large mixing bowl and mix.
2. Place eggs in a separate bowl, mix, and add onion mixture and salt.
3. Heat oil in frying pan and add egg mixture.
4. Fry until bottom part is reddish brown, turn over.

---

[17] http://eggs-recipes.com/hungarian-omelette-recipe/

Ham and Eggs   Frank Hegyi

Ingredients

8 eggs
4 potatoes
8 slices of ham
¼ cup vegetable oil
1 onion cut in small pieces

2 tsp salt
2 tsp pepper
1 tsp paprika
1 tsp ginger
1 tsp onion salt

Ham and Eggs[18]

Instructions

1. Peel potatoes and cook in a microwave oven or in water. When cooked, cut into slices.
2. In a large frying pan, heat oil on medium and sauté onions until golden brown, put in ham, potatoes, season with salt and pepper, cook mixture on medium heat for 15 minutes or until all components are tender.
3. Place eggs in a bowl and beat until liquid is smooth. Season with salt, pepper, paprika, ginger and onion salt. Heat oil in a medium sized frying pan, then place in egg mixture and cook as scrambled eggs.

---

[18] http://allrecipes.com/recipe/240125/sharons-egg-and-ham-scramble/

Recipes of Canadian Martyrs and St. Margaret Mary Church

Potato pancakes   Frank Hegyi

Ingredients

1 onion large grated   6 potatoes peeled and grated
2 tbsp flour   2 eggs
2 tsp salt   ¾ tsp black pepper
1 pint sour cream   ½ cup cream

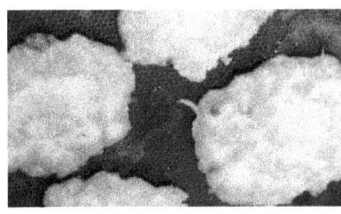

Potato pancakes[19]

Instructions

1. In a large bowl, use a mixer to puree onions, potatoes, flour, eggs, salt and pepper.
2. Heat oil in a skillet and when hot drop large spoonful of the mixture. Cook until browned on one side.
3. Turn and repeat.
4. When done remove, drain and place in a warm oven.
5. Mix the sour cream & cream together. Serve warm with a large dollop of the cream mixture.

---

[19] https://www.reference.com/food/potato-pancakes-

Turkish Poached Eggs   Pamela Dixon
(adapted from Nigella Lawson's Nigella: At My Table)

Ingredients

1 cup of Greek yogurt – unsweetened   1 clove of garlic – minced
1 tsp Salt – sea salt or fleur de sel or other large crystal salt
2 tbsp olive oil   2 tbsp butter
1 tsp red pepper flakes (Aleppo pepper)   Fresh herbs (if you wish)
Egg(s)   Toasted bread (optional but recommended)

Turkish Poached Eggs[20]

Instructions

1. Poach your egg or eggs if you would like more than one.
2. Add your eggs to the yoghurt and drizzle with the chilli oil or chilli paste or salsa or fresh pepper/tomatoes.
3. If you want toast to dip in this egg dish, set bread in the toaster.
4. Chop up a few stems of fresh herbs. Nigella's clip showed dill, but I think you could use parsley or even chives. Add to the yoghurt.
5. Add the toast once it is finished and enjoy!

---

[20]https://www.bing.com/search?q=Poached+Turkish+Eggs&filters=ufn%3a%2 2Poached+Turkish+Eggs

Recipes of Canadian Martyrs and St. Margaret Mary Church

Easy flavour packed Lemonade Pamela Dixon

(from Food Wishes Chef John's foodwishes.com *State Fair*)

Ingredients

6 Lemons 5 cups water
1 ¼ cups white sugar

Easy flavour packed Lemonade[21]

Instructions

1. Wash the lemons. If the lemons are waxy, use hot water and scrub.
2. See a vegetable peeler to remove the peel from the lemons. Chef John does say a bit of pith is fine.
3. Place the lemon peel in a large bowl; add the white sugar. Toss to make sure all the peel is coated in sugar.
4. Cover and let sit for 2 hours or overnight – the longer you let the peel sit in the sugar the more oil will be released from the peel and the more flavourful the lemonade.
5. Place the water in a pot on the stove. Heat on high until the water begins to boil. Once at a boil, turn off the heat.
6. Transfer the lemon peel sugar mixture to the water. Stir. Let sit until all the sugar has completely dissolved. (Make take up to 5 minutes or more).
7. Strain the water, lemon peel solution through a strainer/colander into a bowl. Let the liquid cool to room temperature.
8. Juice the six lemons that were peeled earlier, into the cooled liquid.
9. Adjust the amount of sugar or lemon juice to your taste.
10. Transfer mixture to pitcher and refrigerate.
11. Best served cold. Enjoy!

---

[21] https://kitchencents.com/easy-honey-lemonade/

Recipes of Canadian Martyrs and St. Margaret Mary Church

12. Chef John suggests serving over ice cubes with a slice of lemon.
13. Chef John recommends that the water mixture be at room temperature before adding the lemon juice to maintain the lemon flavour. If the lemon juice is added to the water mixture when it is hot; the heat may break down some of the lemon juice (cooking it).

Recipes of Canadian Martyrs and St. Margaret Mary Church

Cranberry Pancakes — Mike Charrier

Ingredients

1 1/3 cups flour	2 tbsp sugar
2 tsp baking powder	3/4 tsp salt
1 1/4 cups milk	1 egg
1 tbsp melted shortening or salad oil	
Handful frozen cranberries halved	

Cranberry Pancakes[22]

Instructions

1. Mix pancakes then add the cranberries. Mix well. Cook on hot griddle in size you like.
2. We had made these pancakes for years, easy and fast. Then our son suggested adding the cranberries and they gave an added zest to the breakfast.

---

[22] https://www.bing.com/search?q=Cranberry+Orange+Pancake+Muffins&filters=ufn%3a%22Cranberry+Orange+Pancake+Muffins

Recipes of Canadian Martyrs and St. Margaret Mary Church

Soups

Angie Davis

Mike Charrier

Kelly Beaton

Recipes of Canadian Martyrs and St. Margaret Mary Church

Gulyas Soup (Gulyás leves) — Frank Hegyi

Ingredients

2 medium sized onions
2 oz. vegetable oil
1 lb stewing beef
1 garlic clove
3 potatoes
1 medium sized tomatoes

3 tbsp Hungarian paprika
1 tsp caraway seed
1 tsp marjoram
1 tsp table salt
1 tsp dill
1 tsp ground pepper 1 carrot

Gulyas soup[23]

Instructions

1. Warm oil in a pot on medium heat. Put in chopped onions and sauté until light brown. Put in Hungarian paprika, garlic and 1 cup water and stir.
2. Put in chopped up beef (1" cubes) and stir. Put in water to cover the meat about 1 inch above. Cook for 45 minutes on medium heat, add water as needed to keep the meat covered.
3. Season with salt, marjoram, caraway seed, ground pepper and dill. Put in tomatoes (sliced), Pepper and potatoes (cut in 1" cubes).
4. Cook on medium heat for 45 minutes or until meat is tender, season further if needed.

---

[23]https://en.wikipedia.org/wiki/List_of_Hungarian_dishes#/media/File:Hungarian_goulash_soup.jpg

Borsc (Ukrainian)   Rose Hegyi

Ingredients

4 medium red beets cut in strips   10 cups of water or chicken broth
1 medium onion, chopped   1 tsp salt
2 carrots, chopped   1 tsp ground pepper
1 cup white beans   3 tbsp butter
1 small can tomato soup   2 tbsp dill chopped
3 medium potatoes thinly sliced

Borsch[24]

Instructions

1. Soak beans overnight.
2. In a large pot, put in beets, potatoes, onions, carrots and water. Cook until vegetables are tender.
3. Next, add beans and tomato soup and season to taste with salt and pepper.
4. Add butter and stir. Cook for another 5 minutes on medium heat. May add spoonful of sour cream before serving, if desired.

---

[24]https://www.reference.com/food/good-recipe-borscht-soup-15c0c55f2e2c9c51?aq=simple+borscht+soup+recipe

Recipes of Canadian Martyrs and St. Margaret Mary Church

Black Bean Soup   Dianne Borg

Ingredients

1 tbsp. olive oil
2 cans black beans, rinsed
2 medium onions, chopped
Big handful of cilantro, chopped
800-900 ml. chicken broth
1/2 tsp. cayenne

1 red pepper, chopped
1 tbsp. chili powder
1 tbsp. paprika
2 cloves of garlic chopped
1/2 tsp. chili flakes (optional)

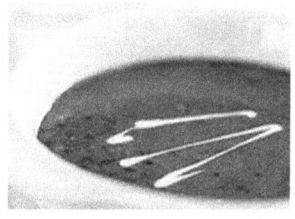

Back bean soup[25]

Instructions

1. Add garlic, red pepper, black beans, cilantro and chicken broth, followed by spices.
2. Bring to boil. Reduce and simmer for 10-15 minutes.
3. Using an immersion blender, purée until soup is smooth. Add more chicken broth if soup is too thick.
4. Serve with some cheese or cilantro on top.

---

[25] http://www.kraftcanada.com/recipes/cuban-black-bean-soup-

Thai Shrimp Soup   Pamela DiNardo

Ingredients

1 tsp fresh lime juice	3 garlic cloves, minced
1 tbsp minced peeled fresh ginger	½ tsp ground coriander
1 tbsp reduced sodium soy sauce	¼ tsp cayenne
1 tsp packed light brown sugar	1 tsp Asian sesame oil
6 cups fish or vegetable broth	2 tbsp chopped fresh cilantro

½ lb fresh white mushrooms sliced
6 oz thin dried Chinese noodles or capellini
1 lb medium shrimp peeled   2 scallions thinly sliced and deveined
¼ lb fresh snow peas trimmed and sliced diagonally in half

Thai Shrimp Soup[26]

Instructions

1. Combine the lime juice, ginger, soy sauce, sugar, oil, garlic, coriander, and cayenne in a small bowl. Set the mixture aside, at room temperature, to allow the flavors to blend at least 15 minutes or up to 2 days. Meanwhile bring the broth to a boil in a Dutch oven.
2. Add the noodles and simmer, uncovered until almost tender, about 5 minutes.
3. Add the shrimp, mushrooms, and snow peas, return to a boil. Reduce the heat and simmer uncovered, until the shrimp are just opaque in the centre and the vegetables are softened, about 2 minutes
4. Stir the lime juice mixture into the broth, return to a simmer.
5. Serve the soup sprinkled with the scallions and cilantro.

---

[26] https://www.tasteofhome.com/recipes/thai-shrimp-soup

Butter Nut Squash Soup Pamela DiNardo

Ingredients

1 butter nut squash Nutmeg
2 tbsp unsalted butter
Add salt and pepper

1 onion
6 cups of chicken stock

Butter Nut Squash Soup[27]

Instructions

1. Cut squash into 1 inch chunks. In large pot melt butter, add onion and cook until translucent, about 8 minutes. Add squash and stock. Bring to a simmer and cook until squash is tender.
2. Remove squash chunks with slotted spoon and place in a blender and puree.
3. Return blended squash to pot. Stir and season with nutmeg, salt, and pepper.
4. Everyone will think there is cream in this soup as it is so delicious.

---

[27] https://www.wholefoodsmarket.com/recipe/classic-butternut-squash-soup

Recipes of Canadian Martyrs and St. Margaret Mary Church

Roasted Red Pepper Soup   Pamela DiNardo

Ingredients

3 lb Red Bell peppers
1 tbsp extra virgin olive oi
1 tbsp unsalted butter
1 large yellow onion, diced
4 cloves garlic, minced
½ cups broth (chicken or vegetable)

1 bay leaf
½ tsp dried thyme
1 tsp salt
¼ tsp cayenne pepper
¼ cup dry white wine

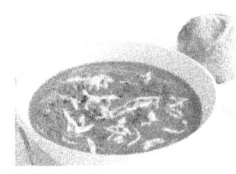

Roasted Red Pepper Soup[28]

Instructions

1. Preheat the oven to 400 degrees and move oven rack to the top rung Half red peppers, take out the seeds and stem. Place skin side up on the rimmed baking sheet
2. Roast for 30-40 minutes until blackened (check after 20)
3. Remove from the oven and immediately cover the pan in foil. Steam for about 10 minutes. Uncover and let the pepper cool. Once cool enough to handle, remove the stem and peel the skin. Set aside.
4. **For the soup**: Add oil and butter in a large pot and heat over medium heat. Once the butter has melted, add in onions and cook until softened, about 5-7 minutes. Add in garlic and let cook for 30 seconds.
5. Add in white wine and cook until most of the wine has been absorbed -1 minute.
6. Now add in the red peppers – if there was some liquid in the bowl, add that too, broth, bay leaf, thyme and cayenne.
7. Bring heat to high, bring to a boil. Cover. Reduce Heat. Simmer for 5 minutes. Remove bay leaf. Blend.

---

[28] http://www.foodnetwork.com/recipes/food-network-kitchen/roasted-red-pepper-soup-recipe-

Chicken/Turkey and Red Lentil Soup — Nancy MacDonald

Ingredients:

1 tbsp extra virgin olive
2 large celery ribs, finely chopped
1½ cloves of garlic, minced
¼ tsp ground ginger
¼ tsp hot pepper flakes

2 carrots, finely chopped
½ large onion, sliced
1 tsp curry powder
¼ tsp ground cumin

Chicken/Turkey and Red Lentil soup[29]

Instructions

1. Heat the oil in a large pot over medium heat. Add all the above. Cover and cook for 15 minutes, stirring occasionally until the vegetables have softened.
2. Stir in ¾ cup of red lentils. Add 5 cups chicken broth. Stir 1 tbsp of tomato paste into a bit of water. Add to the pot.
3. Add 2 pounds of boneless, skinless chicken breasts (or can use leftover cooked chicken or turkey.) Partially cover the pot and simmer for 30 minutes until veg are soft and the chicken is cooked through.
4. Remove the pot from the heat. Remove chicken from pot, place on cutting board and shred or cut up.
5. In a blender or food processor, puree 2 cups of the soup, then return it to the pot, along with the chicken. The soup is done! Serves 6

---

[29] https://www.bing.com/search?q=Leftover+Chicken+Lentil+Soup&filters=ufn%3a%22Leftover+Chicken+Lentil+Soup

Recipes of Canadian Martyrs and St. Margaret Mary Church

Mushroom Pancetta Soup — Nancy MacDonald

Ingredients

3 tbsp butter 1/2 c. Finely chopped celery
1/2 cup peeled and finely chopped shallots 1 and 1/2 tsps. salt
1 tsp pepper 6 cups chicken stock
1 cup sour cream 2 tbsp cognac (opt.)
4 oz pancetta, finely chopped 2 lbs cremini mushrooms finely sliced
1/2 cup finely chopped flat leaf parsley (option)

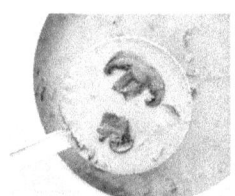

Mushroom Pancetta Soup[30]

Instructions

1. In a large pot over medium high heat, melt the butter and sauté the shallots and celery until soft, about 10 minutes. Add the pancetta and cook for another five minutes, until it is just beginning to crisp. Add the sliced mushrooms, parsley, salt, and pepper and continue to cook until the mushrooms have softened and begin to break down, about 15 minutes.
2. Whisk together the chicken stock and sour cream and add it to the pot. Stir to combine. Bring the soup to a boil, then reduce the heat and allow it to simmer for about 15 minutes.
3. Set a large measuring cup to scoop up half the soup mixture and transfer it to a blender to purée. Returning to the pot and stir to combine add the cognac and stir again. Season with more salt and pepper if you feel it needs it.
4. Store covered in the refrigerator for several days. Should you want to freeze it I suggest you do not add the sour cream until you have thawed the soup. Makes 6 servings

---

[30]https://www.bing.com/search?q=Mushroom+Pancetta+Soup&filters=ufn%3a%22Mushroom+Pancetta+Soup

Recipes of Canadian Martyrs and St. Margaret Mary Church

Creamy Carrot Coconut soup — Susan Scott Hanley

Ingredients

1/4 cup unsalted butter   1/2 cup onion, chopped
1/2 tsp salt   1/4 tsp black pepper
1 (13.5 oz) can of full fat coconut milk   1-2 cups water, as desired
2 cups chicken or vegetable broth
1 lb carrots, peeled and chopped into 1/2 inch slices
1 tsp of Chinese or Thai hot chili oil, more as desired

Creamy Carrot Coconut soup[31]

Instructions

1. Melt butter in a large saucepan over medium heat. Add carrots and onions, and cook until softened, 15 minutes.
2. Stir in broth, coconut milk, salt, pepper, and hot sauce and bring to a boil. Lower the heat and simmer for 40 minutes until very soft.
3. Remove from heat and cool for 15minutes. Blend mixture in a blender until smooth.
4. Rinse out saucepan and return the soup to the pan. Add water until the soup reaches the desired consistency. Taste the soup and add more hot chili oil and salt if desired.
5. Reheat and serve.

This low carb cream of carrot soup is the perfect blend of carrots, coconut milk and hot chili oil. And each nutrient rich bowl has just 8g net carbs.
Prep Time: 25 Cook Time: 55 Total Time: 1 hour20 minutes
Yield: 5 – 6 cups Author: Resolution Eats.

---

[31] https://www.bing.com/search?q=Carrot+Coconut+Soup&filters=ufn%3a%22 Carrot+Coconut+Soup

Recipes of Canadian Martyrs and St. Margaret Mary Church

Garlic Soup (Vegetarian) Fr. Tim Coonen

Ingredients

12 cloves of garlic. well minced
6 cups water
2 vegetable bouillon cubes
8 slices French bread, diced
8 oz tomato sauce or peeled tomatoes

1/2 cup olive oil
l bay leaf
2 well-beaten eggs
salt and pepper
a pinch of cayenne (optional)

Garlic Soup

Instructions

1. In a soup pot, sauté garlic in olive oil over low heat without allowing it to brown or burn. Stir continuously. Add 3 cups water, the bouillon cubes, and the tomato sauce. Stir well.
2. Add remaining water, the French bread, bay leaf, salt and pepper to taste. Bring to a boil, stirring continually, then reduce heat and let cook for about 15 minutes.
3. Simmer slowly for another 15 minutes.
4. In a deep bowl beat the 2 eggs gently, adding half a cup of the soup to it and blending the mixture very well. Pour this mixture slowly into the soup, stirring constantly. Simmer for another 2 minutes. Serve hot.

Note: This is a very popular dish in Spain and southern France, where one can find as many variations of this basic soup as there are households. piping hot garlic soup is particularly appetizing on a cold winter day. (4-6 servings)
I found this recipe in a French monastery vegetarian cookbook; it's terrific. I've since brought it to a parish clean-up event, where it was a big hit, even for non-vegetarians!

Pea Soup   Barb Popel

Ingredients

500 g green split peas   1-2 lbs pork hocks
1 celery root, peeled   1 bunch of leeks, sliced
200 g smoked sausage, sliced   4 carrots, chopped
salt and pepper to taste

Pea Soup[32]

Instructions

1. Soak the peas for 3 to 4 hours or overnight.
2. Drain. Boil the pork with celery root in 3 liters of water until done.
3. Take the pork and celery root out of the broth and add water until you again have 3 liters of water. Stir in the peas and bring to boil, reduce the heat and stir often until the peas are tender (approximately 2 hours).
4. Add mashed up celery root and the pork meat, sliced leeks and carrots. Add salt and pepper to taste. Just before serving, add sliced sausages.

---

[32] https://www.bing.com/search?q=Pea+Soup2

Recipes of Canadian Martyrs and St. Margaret Mary Church
Cold Cranberry Soup — Gina Downing

Ingredients

2 oranges
1 tbsp butter
1 1/4 cup sugar
1 cup sherry
1 pecan halves

1 lb. fresh or frozen cranberries
1 cup light cream
1 cup sour cream
1 cup club soda

Cold Cranberry Soup[33]

Instructions

1. Peel the oranges and cut rind into very fine julienne strips. Squeeze the orange and reserve the juice. Melt butter in a saucepan and sauté the orange rind. Do not brown!
2. Add sugar, sherry, and orange juice and boil for 2 minutes.
3. Add cranberries and cover, boil for 2 minutes. Uncover and boil for another 3 minutes. This mixture may be made a day in advance and chilled overnight. After the mixture is chilled, put in a blender and add the sauterne.
4. Blend at moderate speed for 1 minute. Add the light cream and sour cream and blend for another minute. Strain to remove any cranberry seed or orange rind from the mixture. Before serving add the club soda and mix well.
5. Chill well and serve on ice. Garnish with 2 pecan halves per cup. 8 servings

---

[33] https://www.bing.com/search?q=Chilled+Raspberry+Soup&filters=ufn%3a%22Chilled+Raspberry+Soup

Recipes of Canadian Martyrs and St. Margaret Mary Church

Cabbage Soup   Della Dupuis

Ingredients

1 large onion, chopped	3 tbsp oil
½ cup celery, chopped	2 tsp salt
½ cup green pepper, chopped	2 tbsp sugar
1 lb ground beef, medium	¼ tsp pepper
1 can (28 oz) whole tomatoes	½ tsp paprika
2 cans (5½ oz) tomato paste	2 beef bouillon cubes
2-4 chilli pepper or flakes	3 tbsp chopped parsley
2 cups diced potatoes	1 cup diced carrots
1 small head cabbage, chopped	3 tbsp Parmesan cheese

Cabbage Soup[34]

Instructions

1. Heat oil in a large pot, add onions, celery and green pepper and sauté.
2. Add ground beef and cook until redness is gone.
3. Add salt, sugar, pepper, paprika, tomatoes, tomato paste, 4 cups of hot water, beef bouillon cubes, chilli pepper, parsley, potatoes and carrots. Cook for 1 hour.
4. Add cabbage and cook for another hour, add water as required but keeping soup thick and hearty. Serve in soup bowls and sprinkle with parmesan cheese. 8 servings

---

[34]https://www.bing.com/search?q=Cabbage+Soup&filters=ufn%3a%22Cabbage+Soup

Chicken Broth "pour le rhume" Elaine Borg

Ingredients

1 large pot chicken bones
1-2 chopped onions
2 whole peeled garlic cloves
2 inch piece of ginger
1 skinny green finger pepper

2 bay leaves
1 tsp thyme
1 tsp sage
1 stalk lemongrass
3 carrots and celery

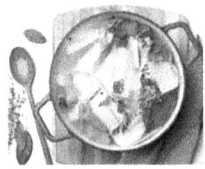

Chicken Broth[35]

Instructions

1. Make chicken stock by adding to large pot chicken bones, chopped onion, chopped carrot, chopped celery, 2 bay leaves, thyme and sage. Add at least enough water to cover the bones. Bring to a boil then simmer for 1.5 hours. Strain, discarding all but the broth. Let broth cool, then refrigerate overnight so that any fat can be easily skimmed from the surface.
2. To prepare broth for your patient, for every litre (4 cups) of the chicken stock you are using, add 2 whole, peeled garlic cloves, 2 inch piece of ginger, unpeeled and cut into chunks, one stalk lemongrass (to use, slice the bottom couple of inches as you would a green onion and discard the long tough parts which comprise the majority of its length) and one skinny green finger pepper, pierced several times.
3. Bring all of this to a boil, then simmer for ½ hour.
4. Strain and discard the flavour sources so you are left with a clear bbroth. Serve immediately so it is very hot, with liberal sprinkling of salt if desired.

---

[35]https://www.bing.com/search?q=Chicken+Broth&filters=ufn%3a%22Chicken+Broth Zdunich

Recipes of Canadian Martyrs and St. Margaret Mary Church

Polish Mushroom Soup — Debbie & Chris Kuchciak

Ingredients
- 1 package (5 oz) dried mushrooms
- 12 shitake mushrooms
- 3 quarts beef stock
- 5 ribs celery chopped
- 2 large onions chopped
- 1 cup sour cream
- 4 tbsp fresh dill finely chopped
- 5 carrots chopped
- 1 lb white mushrooms
- 1 can orzo (pasta)
- 2 tbsp butter
- 2 tbsp flour
- 2 tbsp fresh parsley chopped
- Salt and ground pepper

Polish Mushroom Soup[36]

Instructions

1. Rinse dried mushrooms well in a sieve and soak overnight in 2 cups cold water. Bring stock to a simmer, add celery, onions and carrots. Strain dried mushrooms, reserve the liquid they were soaked in and add to the simmering stock.
2. Chop hydrated mushrooms into 1/4" chunks and add to stock. Slice white mushrooms and add to the stock. Cover and cook soup until the vegetables are tender about an hour. Bring soup to a boil, stirring constantly and add the orzo - reduce heat to a gentle boil and stir occasionally to prevent sticking about 6 to 8 minutes.
3. Make a roux: melt butter in a small saucepan over medium heat, add flour and cook stirring constantly about 3-5 minutes. Remove 1 cup of broth from the soup and add to the roux whisking constantly until thickened and free of lumps. Stir thickened liquid into soup.
4. Add parsley, dill, salt and pepper and reduce heat to low for another 5 to 10 minutes. Allow soup to cool and add sour cream to the soup, stir until well incorporated (if soup isn't given a chance to cool the sour cream will separate).

---

[36] https://www.bing.com/search?q=Polish+Mushroom+Soup&filters=ufn%3a%22Polish+Mushroom+Soup

Minestrone soup   Gen Gales

Ingredients

1 onion finely sliced
3 carrots, sliced
3 stalks celery, sliced
1 small zucchini, diced
4-5 green beans cut in small pieces
¾ cup small pasta (shells)
1 can (19oz) white kidney beans, drained (optional)
½ cup chopped fresh parsley
Salt and pepper
1 potato, peeled and sliced
3 cloves garlic, diced
6 cups chicken stock
28 oz. can of tomatoes undrained, chopped
1 tsp dried oregano and basil
1 cup freshly grated Parmesan cheese
Dash hot pepper sauce

Minestrone soup[37]

Instructions

1. In large saucepan, sauté onion, carrots, celery, zucchini, potato, green beans and garlic in small amount of butter for a few minutes.
2. Add tomatoes. Bring to a boil.
3. Add chicken stock, bring to boil.
4. Add pasta, oregano and basil; cook for 10 to 12 minutes or until pasta is tender but firm and vegetables are cooked.
5. Add kidney beans, parsley, Parmesan cheese and hot pepper sauce; heat through.
6. Season with salt and pepper to taste. 8 servings

---

[37] https://www.bing.com/search?q=Minestrone+Soup&filters=ufn%3a%22Mine strone+Soup22+

Cioppino Soup
Danielle LeBanne

Ingredients

1/4 cup olive oil
1 large onion, chopped
1 red pepper finely chopped
3 garlic cloves, minced
7 ½ oz can tomato sauce
¼ tsp ground black pepper
2 lbs mussels, scrubbed

8 oz bottle clam juice
1 cup dry red wine
2 cups chicken broth or bouillon
1 tsp dried basil
¼ tsp leaf oregano
1 tsp Tabasco sauce
½ lb large shrimp, shelled

Cioppino Soup[38]

Instructions

1. Heat oil over medium heat. Add onion, red pepper and garlic and sauté for about 5 minutes or until the onion is soft.
2. Add the other ingredients (minus the mussels and shrimp) and bring to a boil, then cover, reduce the heat and simmer for 20 minutes.
3. Stir in mussels and simmer, covered, for 2 to 3 minutes.
4. Then stir in shrimp and simmer, covered, for 2 to 3 more minutes or until pink in color. Taste and season with salt and pepper. Discard and mussels that do not open.
5. Serve soup along with a warm crusty bread

---

[38]https://www.bing.com/search?q=Cioppino&filters=ufn%3a%22Cioppino%22

Golden Carrot Soup — Alana Forrester-Verge

Ingredients ion

¼ cup (50ml) butter
1 small minced clove garlic (optional)
2 ½ cups sliced carrots
2 tbsp chicken bouillon mix

1 sliced medium onion
5 cups water
¼ cup long grain rice
salt and chopped parsley

Golden Carrot Soup[39]

Instructions

1. Melt butter in medium saucepan. Sauté onion and garlic until tender.
2. Add water, carrots, rice and bouillon mix.
3. Bring to boil. Cover and simmer 20 to 25 min.
4. Spoon vegetable mixture, part at a time, into blender container.
5. Cover and blend until smooth.
6. Add salt and parsley to taste. May use vegetarian bouillon instead of water, canola oil instead of butter, brown rice instead of white.

---

[39] https://www.bing.com/search?q=Golden+Carrot+Soup+with+Mozzarella&filters=ufn%3a%22Golden+Carrot+Soup+with+Mozzarella

Dill Pickle (Ogorki) Soup   Frank Cedar

Ingredients

3 or 4 potatoes　　　　　　　　1 or 2 carrots
1 parsnip　　　　　　　　　　　½ onion
1 clove garlic　　　　　　　　　1 liter chicken broth
2 bay leaves　　　　　　　　　1 tbsp dill
3 dill pickles　　　　　　　　　2 tbsp flour
3 tbsp sour cream　　　　　　½ cup cream

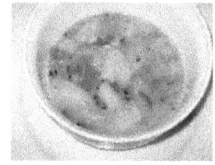

Dill Pickle (Ogorki) Soup[40]

Instructions

1. Dice potatoes into cubes. Shred and/or dice carrots. Dice parsnip, garlic and onion.
2. Cook above in chicken broth in a pot for approx 30 minutes. (Water can be added to thin the soup).
3. Season with pepper. bay leaves, parsley, dill and salt. Mix flour in cold water.
4. Add sour cream and mix. Add this mixture to soup. Add cream.
5. Dice and shred dill pickles and add to soup.
6. Add 2 tbsp liquid from dill pickle bottle.

---

[40] https://www.thespruceeats.com/pickle-soup-from-gwizdaly-village-recipe-

Recipes of Canadian Martyrs and St. Margaret Mary Church

Dutch Pea Soup   Theresa and Cornel Bierman

Ingredient

2 ¼ cup split green peas
2 smoked ham hocks
¾ cups diced carrots
1 small celery root diced
2 leeks sliced thin, white parts
1 tsp pepper

10 cups water
2 ½ cups diced peeled potatoes
¾ cups chopped celery
1 cup chopped onions
1 tsp salt

Dutch Pea Soup[41]

Instructions

1. In large pot bring water and ham hocks to boil and simmer for a 1½ hours.
2. Remove hocks and let liquid cool overnight. De-fat liquid. Trim off fat from hocks; discard.
3. Cut meat from bone, slice and reserve. Reheat liquid with peas to boil. Simmer for 2 minutes. Remove from heat, cover and let stand one hour.
4. Add vegetables; simmer covered for 2 hours.
5. Add reserved meat, salt and pepper to taste. Soup should be fairly thick. If soup seems too thick, thin with hot water or chicken bouillon when reheating.

---

[41] https://www.thespruceeats.com/traditional-dutch-split-pea-soup-

Old Fashioned Pea Soup
Lisa Sheehy

Ingredients

1 ½ cups dry yellow split peas
2 cans(10 oz) chicken broth
1 cup shredded carrot
1 cup chopped celery
3 cups milk
1 tsp pepper
1 tsp chopped parsley

2 ½ cups water
2 cups cooked ham
1 cup chopped onion
2 tbsp butter
1 tsp salt
1 small package croutons

Old Fashioned Pea Soup[42]

Instructions

1. Wash peas and place in a large saucepan.
2. Add water, condensed chicken broth,
3. 1 cup of ham coarsely chopped, carrots, onion, celery and butter.
4. Bring to a boil, then simmer, covered, for 2 - 2½ hours, or until peas are tender.
5. Stir in milk and remaining ham.
6. Add salt and pepper. Reheat to serving temperature. Garnish with croutons and parsley.

---

[42] https://www.todaysparent.com/recipe/soups/old-fashioned-split-pea-soup/

Poultry

Janice Cameron

Susan Scott Handley

Louise Blanchet Smith

Recipes of Canadian Martyrs and St. Margaret Mary Church

Hungarian chicken paprikás   Frank Hegyi

Ingredients

2 medium sized onions
2 oz. vegetable oil
3-4 lbs chicken pieces
1 cup sour cream
1 medium sized tomato
1 cup flour

3 tbsp. Hungarian paprika
1 tsp caraway seed
1 tsp marjoram
1 tsp table salt
1 tsp dill
1 tsp ground pepper

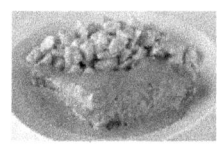

Hungarian Chicken Paprikás[43]

Instructions

1. Warm oil in a pot, put in chopped up onions and sauté until light brown. Add Hungarian paprika and stir. Pour in 1 cup water and add chicken pieces.
2. Pour in more water until chicken pieces are covered. Cook on medium heat for 30 minutes. Add tomato cubes and season with salt, pepper, paprika, caraway seed, marjoram and dill. Cook until chicken is done.
3. Remove chicken pieces into a large pot, using a slotted spoon
4. Mix sour cream and flour in a small bowl with 3 tbsp. of liquid from the cooked chicken until this mixture is smooth. Pour this into the large pan containing the liquid after the chicken pieces are removed, boil it on high for 5 minutes while stirring it vigorously.
5. Sieve this liquid over the chicken pieces, using a fine sieve to make sure that the solid particles do not go through. Cook on low heat for another 10 minutes. Serve with nokedli.

---

[43]https://en.wikipedia.org/wiki/List_of_Hungarian_dishes#/media/Fl e:Paprikahuh n.jpg

Hungarian Wienerschnitze   Frank Hegyi

Ingredients

2 lbs boneless chicken breasts
400 g seasoned bread crumbs
400 g flour
3 eggs
1 litre vegetable oil

1 tbsp salt
2 tsp pepper
2 tsp onion salt
2 tsp ginger

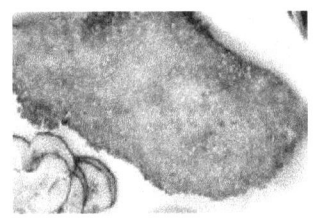

Hungarian Wienerschnitze

Instructions

1. Cut pieces in half and remove fat. Season chicken pieces individually with salt, pepper, onion salt and ginger.
2. Beat eggs in a bowl, season with salt, pepper and onion salt. Place it on a plate. On separate plates, put flour and bread crumbs
3. Dip each chicken piece, both sides, in flour, then in eggs and finally in bread crumbs. Put aside in a separate plate
4. In a deep frying pan, best to use an electric one, heat oil. Place 3-4 chicken pieces in the hot oil. Cook until the bottom side of each chicken piece is slightly brown, turn over each piece and finish cooking.
5. Remove the chicken pieces into a roast pan and finish cooking the remaining pieces in the same way.
6. Once all chicken pieces are cooked, place roast pan in the oven at 150 F and cook for 20 minutes. Then remove from roast pan and place chicken in a serving dish. Serve with Nokedli or potatoes.

Recipes of Canadian Martyrs and St. Margaret Mary Church

Turkey, Spinach and Pasta — Anonymous

Ingredients

6 large turkey sausages
2 cups chicken broth
1 cup shredded cheese

1 14oz can chopped tomatoes
1 large package of spinach

Turkey, Spinach and Pasta[44]

Instructions

1. Cook and brown sausages in a pan. Cool and cut into bite size pieces.
2. Bring the chicken broth and tomatoes to a boil in a large pot or Dutch oven. Add the sausages and pasta.
3. Cook until the pasta is done. Approximate 12 minutes and stir occasionally. Turn down to low. Stir in the spinach, one handful at a time. When this is incorporated, stir in the cheese. Serve.

---

[44] http://www.foodnetwork.com/recipes/giada-de-laurentiis/turkey-and-spinach- taquitos-recipe-2127600

Recipes of Canadian Martyrs and St. Margaret Mary Church

Best Ever Chicken Pate — Pamela DiNardo

Ingredients

1 whole chicken breast boiled
¼ cup chives
3 tsp butter
Fresh parsley

5 tsp mayonnaise
¼ cup cream cheese
1 tsp salt

Chicken Pate[45]

Instructions

1. Boil chicken breast.
2. Combine chives and butter in small container and microwave for 1 minute.
3. Stir in cream cheese.
4. In food processor put chicken, butter and chives cream cheese mixture, mayonnaise and salt. Process until smooth.
5. Pack mixture in a small plastic film lined bowl or mini loaf pan. Chill well, unwrap and garnish with parsley, serve with baguette or crackers.

---

[45]http://ca.zapmeta.com/ws?de=c&q=chicken%20pate%20recipes&asid=ca_ba_gc

Chicken with mushrooms Frank Hegyi

Ingredients

4 oz mushrooms
1 tbsp cornstarch
1 cup skim milk
¼ tsp poultry seasoning
½ tsp ginger
2 cups diced cooked chicken

½ cup green peppers
1 cup low-fat chicken broth
¼ tsp black pepper
¼ cup chopped pimentos
1 tsp fresh parsley
1 tsp paprika

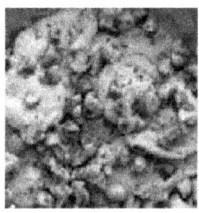

Chicken with Mushrooms[46]

Instructions

1. Coat a non-stick 12-inch skillet with non-stick spray and warm over medium heat.
2. Add the chopped mushrooms, paprika and chopped peppers and sauté until they are softened.
3. Add 1 or 2 tbsp of broth if the vegetables begin to stick. Combine the cornstarch with 1/4 cup of the broth and set aside. Add the remaining broth, milk, black pepper, poultry seasoning, ginger, chicken and pimientos to the skillet.
4. Bring to a boil over medium heat, stirring occasionally. Add the broth mixture and continue cooking until the sauce has thickened. Serve with rice or noodles.

---

[46] https://www.marthastewart.com/925229/chicken-mushrooms

Tomato Slow Cooker Chicken — Pamela DiNardo

Ingredients

4 boneless skinless chicken breasts
2 gloves garlic (finely chopped)
1 ½ tsp dried basil leaves
½ tsp dried oregano leaves
¼ tsp pepper
1 can diced tomatoes drained
1 pouch roasted tomato Mexican cooking sauce
1 jar Alfredo Sauce (15 oz)
2 8 oz. uncooked pasta
½ tsp salt
2 tbsp cornstarch
2 tbsp water

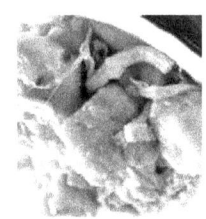

Slow Cooker Chicken[47]

Instructions

1. Spray slow cooker with cooking spray.
2. Arrange chicken breasts on the bottom, top with garlic, basil, oregano, salt and pepper.
3. In a separate bowl, stir together the Alfredo sauce, tomatoes and Mexican cooking sauce until blended. Pour over chicken.
4. Cover and cook on low heat for 5 – 6 hours
5. Ten to 15 minutes before serving time, cook pasta as directed.
6. In small bowl, stir together the cornstarch and water, stir into mixture in slow cooker. Increase heat setting to high; cook uncovered for another 5-10 minutes.
7. Serve chicken with the pasta and top with cheese.

---

[47] http://allrecipes.com/recipes/1203/everyday-cooking/slow-cooker/main-dishes/chicken/

Chicken Thighs with shallots in red wine vinegar (poulet au vinaigre)　　　　　　　　　　　　　　　　　Corry Wink

Ingredients

32 oz (8 lean and trimmed) boneless, skinless chicken thighs
1/2 cup red wine vinegars　　　2 tbsp fresh chopped parsley
kosher salt and fresh pepper　　1 cup chicken broth
1 tbsp honey　　　　　　　　　1 tbsp tomato paste
1 tsp butter　　　　　　　　　　1/2 cup dry white wine
2 tbsp light sour cream　　　　2 cloves garlic, thinly sliced
1 large shallot, thinly sliced (3/4 cup)

Chicken Thighs[48]

Instructions

1. Season the chicken with salt and pepper.
2. In a medium saucepan, combine vinegar, honey, 3/4 cup chicken broth and tomato paste.
3. Boil about 5 minutes, until it reduces down to about 3/4 cup. Remove from heat.
4. In a large skillet, melt butter over medium-low heat and add chicken. Cook on both sides, until brown, about 6-8 minutes. Remove chicken and set aside. Add the shallots and garlic to the skillet and cook on low until soft, about 5 minutes.
5. Pour the sauce over the chicken, add the wine, remaining broth salt and pepper. Cover and simmer about 20 minutes until tender.
6. Remove the chicken, add sour cream and stir into the sauce (if sauce dries up, add more broth).
7. Boil a few minutes then return chicken to skillet. Top with fresh parsley. Total time 35 minutes.

---

[48] https://www.bing.com/search?q=Chicken+in+Red+Wine+Vinegar+Recipe+-+Paula+Wolfert

Recipes of Canadian Martyrs and St. Margaret Mary Church

Amaretto Chicken   Nancy MacDonald

Ingredients

5 boneless skinless chicken breasts cut in large chunks.
Combine the next 5 ingredients and dredge the chicken pieces.
¼ cup flour   1 tsp salt
2 tsp pepper   2 tbsp paprika
1 tbsp garlic salt
Sauté chicken until lightly brown in 2 tbsp butter and 1 tbsp oil. Remove chicken from pan and place in a large casserole dish.
Mix the next 4 ingredients, heat in the same pan and stir until reduced by half.
Pour sauce over chicken.
1 tbsp Dijon mustard   1/4 cup water
¾ cup Amaretto   ½ cup frozen orange juice concentrate

Amaretto Chicken[49]

Instructions

1. Bake covered at 350 for 30 to 35 minutes. Serve with rice.
2. Serves eight for lunch, six for dinner, can be doubled easily.
3. Note: ½ chicken breast per person is more than ample these days. For 4 servings I used 4 halves, reduced the flour mixture by half, reduce the amaretto to ½ cup, but keep the rest of the sauce amounts the same. (Some cooks reduce the paprika)

---

[49]https://www.bing.com/search?q=Amaretto+Chicken+Breast+Holiday+Style&filters=ufn%3a%22Amaretto+Chicken+Breast+Holiday+Style

Recipes of Canadian Martyrs and St. Margaret Mary Church

Spinach and Beet Salad with Chicken   Nancy MacDonald

Ingredients

1 lb. boneless, skinless chicken breast	3 tbsp canola oil
2 tbsp maple syrup	2 tbsp cider vinegar
1 tbsp whole-grain mustard	1 tbsp soy sauce
¼ tsp salt	¼ tsp ground pepper
8 cups baby spinach	½ cup crumbled goat cheese

1 15 oz can whole beets, drained and quartered
¼ cup chopped pecans, toasted (of any chopped nuts, toasted or not)

Spinach and Beet Salad with Chicken[50]

Instructions

1. Place chicken in a skillet and add enough water to cover, bring to a simmer on high heat. Cover, reduce heat and simmer gently until the chicken is cooked through and no longer pink in the middle, 10 to 12 minutes. Transfer the chicken to a cutting board. When cool enough to handle, cut into ¼ inch thick slices.
2. Meanwhile, whisk oil, syrup, vinegar, mustard, soy sauce, salt and pepper in large bowl. Reserve ¼ cup dressing in a small bowl. Add spinach to the large bowl and toss to coat with dressing. Divide the spinach among 4 plates and top with chicken, beets, goat cheese and pecans. Drizzle with reserved dressing.
Makes 4 servings.

---

[50]https://www.bing.com/search?q=Spinach+%26+Beet+Salad+with+Chicken& filters

Recipes of Canadian Martyrs and St. Margaret Mary Church

Cashew Chicken   Paddy Cedar

Ingredients

¼ cup vegetable oil
3 small onions
10 oz of mushrooms
4 chicken breasts, cut-up
10 oz can of water chesnuts
1 cup of vinegar
1 cup of sugar

½ lb snow peas
2 tsp fresh ginger
1 cup of unsalted cashews
2 whole green scallions
½ cup of sherry
2 tbsp soya sauce

Cashew Chicken[51]

Instructions

1   Sauté onions & spread on the bottom of a casserole dish. Layer mushrooms over onions.
2   Stir fry chicken & layer next. Slice & layer water chestnuts. Pour sauce over all & cover. Refrigerate for a day. When ready to serve, place casserole in the oven at 350 F for 30 minutes.
3   Add snow peas, scallions & nuts & bake another 15 minutes. Serve with rice.
    Sauce
4   Add vinegar, sugar, sherry, Soya sauce and fresh ginger, mix together and add green scallions, starch, 2 tbsp water and boil until thickened.
    This sauce is great on spareribs. Parboil ribs, & drain. Brush with soya sauce. bake in a 350 F oven for 1 hour turning occasionally. When brown, pour sauce. Over all, bake another 15 minutes. Serve.

---

[51]https://www.bing.com/search?q=Cashew+Chicken&filters=

Recipes of Canadian Martyrs and St. Margaret Mary Church
Breaded and Baked Chicken   Gen Gales

Ingredients

3 tbsp fresh flat-leaf Parsley   1 cup of breadcrumbs
1 cup of milk   ½ tsp pepper
½ tsp thyme   ¼ cup butter or margarine

Breaded and Baked Chicken[52]

Instructions

1. In a bowl, mix milk, parsley and thyme; set aside. In a plate, mix breadcrumbs and pepper; set aside. Melt butter or margarine, and set aside.
2. Slice chicken breasts lengthwise in two, to obtain thin slices. Dip each slice in the milk mixture, and then roll in breadcrumb mixture. Dip slices in melted butter/margarine, and place in an ovenproof dish.
3. Place slices of onion on top of chicken, and bake at 350 F for approximately 30-40 minutes, depending on thickness of chicken.

---

[52] https://www.bing.com/search?q=Baked+Breaded+Chicken+Strips&filters=uf n%3a%22Baked+Breaded+Chicken+Strips

Recipes of Canadian Martyrs and St. Margaret Mary Church

Chicken and Wild Rice Casserole — Frank Cedar

Ingredients

3 to 4 cups of water
1 cube beef or chicken bouilion
1 cup of wild rice
1 cup chopped onion
1 cup thinly sliced celery
1 ¾ cup of chicken stock
2 tbsp sherry
3 cups of cooked cubed chicken
14 oz can of artichokes, drained and chopped

1 tsp. salt
¾ tsp salt
1 tbsp. butter
¼ cup flour
1 cup shredded carrot
2 cups of light cream
freshly ground pepper
⅓ cup toasted sliced almonds

Chicken and Wild Rice Casserole[53]

Instructions

1 In a medium-sized saucepan, bring water to boil. Add bouillon.
2 Stir in rice and salt. Cover and simmer about an hour, or until rice is tender (popped white). Drain rice in colander. Melt butter in a large frying pan over medium heat.
3 Add onion celery and carrot; cook 10 minutes, stirring occasionally, until softened.
4 Add stock to veggies in frying pan and bring to boil. In bowl, whisk cream and flour until smooth. Gradually whisk into boiling broth. Add salt sherry and pepper. Bring to a boil. Reduce heat and simmer 5 minutes, stirring occasionally. Add rice to the sauce.
5 Add chicken and artichokes to the sauce and mix well. Pour mixture into swallow 2-3 quart (2 to 3 L) baking dish. Cover and bake at 350° F for 35 to 40 minutes or until hot and bubbly. Sprinkle with toasted almonds.

---

[53]https://www.bing.com/search?q=Chicken+and+Wild+Rice+Casserole&filters=ufn%3a%22Chicken+and+Wild+Rice+Casserole

Recipes of Canadian Martyrs and St. Margaret Mary Church
Lemon Glazed Chicken — Gina Downing

Ingredients

¼ tsp. oregano
2 tsp. grated lemon peel
3 tbsp. lemon juice
3 lb broiler fryer chicken

1 ½ tsp. seasoned salt
⅛ tsp. pepper
2 tbsp. butter
½ cup dark corn syrup

Lemon Glazed Chicken[54]

Instructions

1. Add butter to electric skillet, sauté chicken (at 350 F) until golden;
2. Add oregano, lemon, lemon peel, lemon juice, corn syrup, and ½ cup of water.
3. Cover and simmer at 250 F for about 45 minutes or until tender, basting several times with pan drippings. 4 servings

---

[54]https://www.bing.com/search?q=Honey+Glazed+Chicken&filters=ufn%3a%22Honey+Glazed+Chicken

Coq au Vin
Mike MacNeil

Ingredients

1-2 tbsp butter or bacon fat or olive oil
1 tbsp fresh chervil or marjoram
1 garlic clove
4 large pieces chicken
2 tbsp minced parsley
½ tsp thyme
1½ cup dry red wine or sherry
½ bay leaf
1 tbsp fresh chervil or marjoram

¼ cup chopped onions
2 tbsp flour
2 sliced carrots
1-2 tbsp butter or bacon fat
2 tbsp. flour
1 tsp. salt
1-2 tbsp cornstarch
⅛ tsp ground black pepper
½ lb. sliced mushrooms

Coq au Vin[55]

Instructions

1. Brown vegetables lightly in fat/oil. Remove. Brown chicken in fat/oil.
2. Add flour and herbs. Cook.
3. Add vegetables and wine.
4. Simmer 45 minutes.
5. Add mushrooms and cornstarch mixed with a little water; cook 5 minutes longer. 4 servings

---

[55]https://www.bing.com/search?q=Coq+Au+Vin&filters=ufn%3a%22Coq+Au+Vin

Recipes of Canadian Martyrs and St. Margaret Mary Church

Fried Chicken Helen Mitchel

Ingredients

4 chicken breasts
1 cup buckwheat flour
1 tbsp herbes de Provence
¼ tsp sea salt
3 tbsp safflower oil

¼ cup skimmed milk
¼ cup raw sesame seeds
¼ tsp dry mustard
¼ tsp black pepper

Fried Chicken[56]

Instructions

1. Prepare chicken breasts, boneless and skinless, by rinsing in cold running water and drying with paper towels. In a re-sealable bag or on a large plate, measure flour, sesame seeds and seasonings rubbing the herbs de Provence between your palms to release all their flavour. Mix thoroughly.
2. Pour milk in a medium sized bowl. Measure oil in large frying pan and start to heat. Working quickly, individually dip each chicken breast in milk, then completely coat in flour mixture. Gently place in frying pan.
3. Brown each side on medium-high heat, then reduce heat and cook on low, turning frequently to ensure even cooking.
4. Cook until juices run clear - approximately an additional 15 minutes once both sides browned.
5. Serve with mashed potatoes and your favourite colourful veggies.

---

[56]https://www.bing.com/search?q=Skillet+Fried+Chicken&filters=ufn%3a%22Skillet+Fried+Chicken

Meat

Rose Hegyi

Cornelius Kroon

Recipes of Canadian Martyrs and St. Margaret Mary Church
Hungarian Goulash (Pörkölt) Frank Hegyi

Ingredients

2 medium sized onions	3 tbsp. Hungarian paprika
2 oz. vegetable oil	1 tsp caraway seed
3 lbs stewing beef	1 tsp marjoram
1 garlic clove	1 tsp table salt
1 medium green pepper	1 tsp dill
2 medium sized tomatoes	1 tsp ground pepper

The goulash

Instructions

1. Warm oil in a pot on medium heat.
2. Put in chopped up onions and sauté until light brown. Put in Hungarian paprika and stir.
3. Gradually put in chopped up beef and stir.
4. Put in garlic and water to cover the meat. Cook for 45 minutes on medium heat, add water as needed to keep the meat covered.
5. Season by putting in salt, marjoram, caraway seed, ground pepper and dill.
6. Put in tomatoes (cut in cubes) and green pepper (sliced). Cook on medium heat for 45 minutes, make sure water is up to the top of the meat. Cook until meat is tender, season further if needed.
7. Serve with nokedli.

Schnitzel Pork Cutlets Frank Hegyi

Ingredients

2 lbs thin pork cutlets, boneless
2400 g seasoned bread crumbs
400 g flour
3 eggs
1 litre vegetable oil

2 tsbsp salt
2 tbsp pepper
2 tbsp salt
1 tbsp ginger

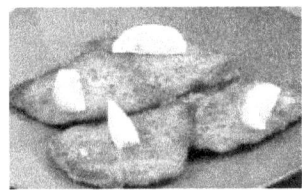

Schnitzel Pork Cutlets[57]

Instructions

1. Cut off fat from pork cutlets. Using mallet, pound each pork cutlet on both sides until thin (¼") and tender.
2. Season both sides with salt, pepper, onion salt and ginger.
3. Beat eggs in a container, season with salt, pepper and onion salt. Place it on a plate.
4. On separate plates, put flour and bread crumbs. Dip each pork cutlet, both sides, in flour, then in eggs and finally in bread crumbs. Put aside in a separate plate.
5. In a deep frying pan, best to use an electric one, heat oil. Place 3-4 cutlets in the hot oil. Cook until the bottom side of the pork is slightly brown, turn over each cutlet, and finish cooking.
6. Remove the cutlets into a roast pan, and finish cooking the remaining cutlets in the same way. Once all cutlets are cooked, place roast pan in the oven at 150 F and cook for 20 minutes. Then remove from roast pan and place in serving dish.

---

[57] http://www.foodnetwork.com/recipes/pork-schnitzel-recipe-2013974

BBQ steak and potatoes — Frank Hegyi

Ingredients

4-T bone steak
6 medium sized potatoes
¼ lb margarine
1 chopped onion
1 tbsp dill

2 tbsp salt
2 tbsp pepper
2 tbsp ginger
2 tbsp marjoram
tin foil

BBQ Steak and Potatoes[58]

Instructions

1. Cut tin foil in sizes that will hold each potato. Clean each potato, and make a cut into it, put in a tsp margarine, onions and season with salt, pepper, ginger, dill, and marjoram. Wrap up each potato in the tin foil and place on BBQ under medium heat. Cook until potatoes appear soft.
2. Wipe each steak with wet paper towel. Season each side with salt, pepper, onion salt and ginger. Place each steak on BBQ on medium heat and cook, turn over several times to ensure that they do not burn. When the insides are only slightly red and the steaks are still juicy, turn heat up to maximum for 2 minutes to seal moisture inside, but ensure that they are not burned.
3. Serve steak with baked potatoes

---

[58] http://allrecipes.com/recipe/256634/grilled-skirt-steak-with-roasted-potatoes/

BBQ Ribs in the Crock Pot — Pamela DiNardo

Ingredients

3 lbs of boneless spare ribs
1 bottle smoke BBQ sauce
1 onion sliced
3 gloves garlic

BBQ Ribs in the Crock Pot[59]

Instructions

1. Sprinkle ribs with salt and pepper. Place ribs under broiler on a pan until browned, up to 15 minutes and remove excess fat.
2. Put sliced onion and minced garlic in crock pot. Slice ribs into serving pieces and put in crock pot, pour BBQ sauce over the top.
3. Cover and cook on low 6 – 8 hours. Add a cup of hot broth mixed with a tablespoon of flour to the bottom of the crock pot during the final hour of cooking if you want a gravy to serve alongside the ribs.
4. I use cumin and brown sugar on the ribs before I brown them as well.

---

[59] http://allrecipes.com/recipe/22230/slow-cooker-barbecue-ribs/

Recipes of Canadian Martyrs and St. Margaret Mary Church
Blue Cheese Crusted Filet Mignon   Pamela DiNardo

Ingredients

4 six ounce filet mignons
Salt and pepper
2 slices whole grain bread, cubed
2 sprigs of fresh rosemary
1 cup red wine   ½ cup heavy cream

Olive Oil
8 oz blue cheese
Half a stick of butter
Fresh ground pepper Pan Sauce

Blue Cheese Crusted Filet Mignon[60]

Instructions

1. Preheat oven to 400
2. Heat a large frying pan over medium high heat. Season the filets and rub with olive oil. Place in the hot pan and sear for 1 minute on each side. Place on a cooling rack fitted over a baking sheet. Reserve the pan.
3. Puree the blue cheese, bread, butter, rosemary and pepper in a food processor until smooth.
4. Pack blue cheese crust onto the tops of the filets and bake in oven until meat is medium-rare, about 8-10 minutes.
5. The meat and crust may be prepared in advance, refrigerated, then baked just before serving. If so add a bit more baking time.
6. Pan Sauce: Add the wine to the searing pan over medium high heat. Scrape loose the brown bits and reduce the wine to a syrup like consistency. Whisk in the cream and continue to reduce until the mixture thickens to a sauce like consistency. Season and serve with the filets

---

[60]ttps://www.omahasteaks.com/buy/Steaks/Fie Mignons?

Toad in the Hole Pamela DiNardo

Ingredients

½ lb flour Pinch of salt
1-2 eggs ½ pint of milk
1 oz of fat drippings
½ pound of sausages (one package of breakfast sausages usually does the trick – about 12 pieces – enough to have them about 1 inch apart in the casserole dish you are using)

Toad in the Hole[61]

Instructions

1 Make a batter with the flour, salt, egg(s) and milk. Same consistency as pancakes. Number of eggs depends on size, two small or 1 large. This can be left to stand until you need it.
2 Heat the olive oil or fat drippings in the casserole dish you are using. Add the batter and drop the sausages all going in one direction about 1 inch apart, one or two rows depending on what you have room for.
3 Bake for 35 minutes at 350 degrees or until browned. Cut into large squares and serve with mashed potatoes and green beans.

---

[61] https://www.bbcgoodfood.com/recipes/1572643/sams-toad-in-the-hole

Recipes of Canadian Martyrs and St. Margaret Mary Church
Marla's Maple Pork — Nancy Macdonald

Ingredients

1 1/2 lbs (680) pork tenderloin
2 tbsp soy sauce and ketchup
2 tsp grated orange zest
1 tsp Worcestershire sauce

1/2 cup maple syrup
1 tbsp Dijon mustard
2 tsp minced garlic
1 1/2 each curry powder and ground coriander

Marla's Maple Pork[62]

Instructions

1. Place pork in resealable plastic bag. Whisk ingredients in medium bowl and pour over pork. Marinate for 1 hour.
2. Transfer pork and marinade to small roasting pan. Roast, uncovered, at 350°F for 40 minutes.
3. Let pork stand for 5 minutes. Slice thinly. Drizzle extra sauce over pork.

---

[62] https://www.ottawacitizen.com/life/Marla+Maple+Pork/5825976/story.html

Bacon Wrapped Pork Loin Corry Wink

Ingredients

1 boneless pork loin (about 1 kg)
3 cloves garlic
½ bunch thyme or 1tbsp dried
1 tsp olive oil
1 sprigs rosemary or 1 tbsp dried

1 lb sliced bacon
2 tsp Dijon mustard
1 tsp dried marjoram
Salt and pepper to taste

Bacon Wrapped Pork Loin[63]

Instructions

1. Mix garlic, dried herbs, salt, pepper, and olive oil. Rinse pork and pat dry.
2. Roll pork in mustard and then in herb mixture which has been laced on a cutting board.
3. Wrap bacon around the pork loin and tuck in loose ends. Wrap tightly in saran wrap and put in fridge for 2-24 hours.
4. Preheat oven to 350. Unwrap pork and put it on a roasting rack and put water or chicken stock in roasting pan to keep meat moist.
5. This liquid can be used to make gravy. Bake uncovered for 2 hours, broiling it for the last 5 minutes to crisp the bacon. Let rest for 5-10 minutes before slicing

Serves 6

---

[63] https://www.bing.com/search?q=Bacon-Wrapped+Pork+Tenderloin&filters

Recipes of Canadian Martyrs and St. Margaret Mary Church

Homemade Kebab and Salad — Pamela Dixon
Refikas Kitchen – Turkish Cuisine Easy Homemade Shish Kebab

Ingredients

250 g ground beef (You could also consider using lamb. Refika suggests using the grind of meat that you use to make hamburgers either lean or medium, your choice)
1 chilli pepper (optional)   1/3 red bell pepper
2 cloves of garlic   1 tbsp red pepper flakes (optional)*
1 tsp salt
1/3 green bell pepper or 4 mild finger sized green peppers or 4 spicy finger sized green peppers – your choice*you could substitute the red pepper flake with zatar seasoning if you have it available
Skewers – either metal or wooden. If using wooden, soak the skewers.
Salad ingredients
2 red onions   7-8 sprigs of parsley
Pinch of salt   2 tbsp olive oil
1.5 tbsp sumac
Serve with flat bread like lavash or tortilla or pita.

Homemade Kebab and Salad[64]

Instructions

1. Chop chilli pepper (if using), red bell pepper and green bell pepper. They should be finely minced. Finely mince the garlic. You can combine the peppers and garlic and mince again. Add the red pepper flakes or zatar seasoning, if using. Add the salt to the pepper/garlic mix. Add the ground meat to the pepper/garlic mixture and combine either by kneading or using your knife to mix.

---

[64] https://www.bing.com/search?q=Healthy+Homemade+Kebabs&filters=ufn%3a%22Healthy+Homemade+Kebabs

2. The meat mixture is now placed on the skewers. Divide into four, two for each person. Form each quarter of the mixture into sausage like shapes and run the skewer up the middle, leaving 1 inch from each end of the skewer. The kebab should be more flat than cylindrical on the skewer. If the meat mixture seems to be falling apart, you can chill it for 20-30 minutes and try again. I found even after chilling, my kebab would not stay on the skewer; so, I just made sausage shapes and cooked them without the skewer. The skewers used in the video were wide metal plates, which I think helped spread the meat around it, rather than a thin pencil shape. Refika suggests you could use wooden craft sticks, tongue depressor size.
3. In the video the kebabs skewers are placed over a cast iron pan heating on the stove. The meat is being cooked via indirect heat and is rotated every minute for approximately 6-7 minutes. This is the traditional way of cooking kebabs in Turkey. However, mine were not on a skewer, so I just cooked them in the cast iron pan. The cast iron pan should be very hot if you are doing indirect heat. You want the meat to brown all the way through. You will need the fan on, so the smoke detector does not go off, the meat will drop juices in the hot pan, and it will smoke. The kitchen will smell heavenly. If you are not using skewers, you may only need 5 minutes to cook through.

Salad prep:
4. Slice the red onion in half and then make thin half rounds. Chop up the parsley. Combine the onions and parsley in a bowl. Add the salt and massage the parsley and onion together. Add the olive oil and sumac. Give the salad a stir.
5. To eat, take your flat bread, place the meat in the middle, add a spoon or two of the salad. Wrap up the bread and enjoy!

Shish Kebab ingredients (for two people)

Recipes of Canadian Martyrs and St. Margaret Mary Church

Souvlaki
Gina Downing

Ingredients

5 lbs pork shoulder,
1 cup oil
1 tsp. crushed garlic
1 tsp. dried mint

1/4 cup vinegar or lemon juice
1 tsp. salt
1 tsp. paprika
1 tsp. oregano

Souvlaki[65]

Instructions

1. In large bowl, combine vinegar (or lemon juice), oil, and spices.
2. Add meat cut in 1" cubes. Cover and refrigerate for 24 - 48 hours. To cook, skewer meat and broil or barbecue for 5 minutes.
3. Serve with Tzadziki sauce a rice pilaf, and a green salad, or, put broiled meat into a pita bread, add shredded lettuce, onion, tomatoes, and Tzadziki sauce.

Tzadziki Sauce For Souvlaki

1 ½ cups sour cream (or ½ plain yogurt)   tbsp. oil
tbsp. white vinegar   ½ tsp. salt
½ tsp. dried mint   2 cloves garlic, crushed
1 small cucumber, "juiced" (cut in half or thirds and juice as you would an orange)2
Mix all ingredients together. Let stand, refrigerated, overnight. 8 servings

---

[65] https://www.bing.com/search?q=Souvlaki&filters=ufn%3a%22Souvlaki

Recipes of Canadian Martyrs and St. Margaret Mary Church

Lillian's Meat Balls   Gen Gales

Ingredients

1½ lb. minced steak
½ lb. minced pork
1 egg
1 tbs. Worchestershire sauce
Salt
⅓ cups of crumbs
2 tbsp instant onion flakes
Drop of Tabasco sauce

Lillian's Meat Balls[66]

Insructions

1 Mix ingredients and roll into 1¼ inch balls.
2 Place in oven at 500° for 5-6 minutes.

Sauce

⅓ cup brown sugar
3 tbsp. fresh lemon juice
8 oz. can of tomato sauce
¼ tsp. garlic salt
2 tbsp. cornstarch
1 cup dry wine (Montmessin)
½ cup of water

Bring to boil and simmer for approximately ½ hour. Pour over meatballs and simmer in oven at 250° - 300° for approximately 2 hours.

---

[66] https://www.bing.com/search?q=Energy+Balls&filters2

Recipes of Canadian Martyrs and St. Margaret Mary Church

Beef Hot Pot   Sheila Gasnick

Ingredients

1 lb stewing steak   ¾ pint stock or water
1 oz flour   1 tsp salt
4 onions   1 tsp pepper
1½ lb potatoes   Shavings of drippings
Sprigs of parsley

Beef Hot Pot[67]

Instructions

1. Cut the meat into small pieces and toss in seasoned flour to coat them.
2. Slice the onions and put them into a casserole, place the meat on top and the peeled potatoes cut in thick slices or quarters.
3. Pour in the stock or water and dot the surface of the potatoes with a few shavings of dripping.
4. Add salt and pepper. Cover and bake in a moderate oven at 375 F for about 2 hours or until the meat is tender. Remove the lid for the past 20 minutes of the baking time so that the potatoes brown on top.
5. Garnish with parsley sprigs.

---

[67] https://www.bing.com/search?q=Beef+Hotpot&filters=

Quiche Lorraine — Barb Popel

Ingredients

1 cup ham
2 tbsp flour
¾ cup milk
1 large pre-baked pie shell
1 small onion, chopped

½ lb. cheese, grated
¾ cup table cream
1 tsp nutmeg
3 eggs, lightly beaten

Quiche Lorraine[68]

Instructions

1 Stir flour into eggs. Combine egg mixture, cream, milk and nutmeg.
2 Put chopped cooked ham, onion and cheese (Emmenthal or Jarlsberg) into the pre-baked pie shell(s). Cover this with the milk mixture, ensuring that all ingredients are covered (add more milk if necessary).
3 Bake at 350 F for 20 to 25 minutes, until golden brown. If the crust is brown but the contents are still liquid, turn down or turn off the oven.
4 Let the pie sit for 5 minutes before serving it.

---

[68] https://www.bing.com/search?q=Quiche+Lorraine&filters=ufn%3a%22Quiche+Lorraine

Norma's Sparerib
Barb Popel

Ingredients

3 strips of pork baby back ribs
1 cup brown sugar
2 tbsp celery seed
2 onions, sliced

2 tins tomato soup
1 cup. white vinegar
2 tbsp. chili powder

Norma's Sparerib[69]

Instructions

1. Cook ribs in oven at 375 F for about 30 minutes.
2. Mix the rest of the ingredients in a pot, warm this, pour over the ribs, and bake for about 1 hour. Stir.
3. Bake another hour, covering with foil when they are brown enough.

---

[69]https://www.tasteofhome.com/recipes/herbed-spareribs/

Beef Tourtiere Joanne Robichaud

Ingredients

1 lb beef hamburger
1 lb pork hamburger
1 small onion finely chopped
1-2 cup boiling water
Pastry for two 10 inch pies

1 clove of garlic
1 tsp clove
1 tsp salt
1 tsp cinnamon
¼ tsp pepper

Beef Tourtiere[70]

Instructions

1. Mix together meat and spices in a large pot.
2. Add water and cook at medium to low heat until meat has lost its pink colour.
3. Once cooked, cool for the meat mixture. Prepare pastry. Put meat mixture in pie plates.
4. Cook pies at 350 F for 1 hour

---

[70] https://www.bing.com/search?q=Tourtiere&filters=ufn

Recipes of Canadian Martyrs and St. Margaret Mary Church
Moroccan Chicken Stew — Lisa Sheehy

Ingredients

1¼ lb boneless skinless chicken
2 cups water
1 tsp tumeric,
1 tsp granulated sugar
1 sweet potato, peeled and cubed
1 cup canned or cooked chick-peas
1 tbsp lemon juice
2 tbsp chopped fresh parsley or cilantro

3 cups onions, thinly sliced
1 tbsp minced gingerroot
1 tsp cinnamon
½ tsp saffron (optional)
4 carrots, cut in chunks
¼ cup dried currants
1 small zucchini chunks
1 ½ cups couscous

Moroccan Chicken Stew[71]

Instructions

1. In non stick skillet or saucepan, brown chicken cut in cubes over high heat; remove chicken to plate and set aside.
2. Reduce heat to medium and add onions; cook, stirring occasionally, for about 5 minutes or until softened.
3. Add water, gingerroot, turmeric, cinnamon, sugar and saffron; bring to a simmer.
1. Add sweet potato and carrots; cover and simmer for 20 minutes. Add chick-peas, currants and lemon juice. Recipe can be prepared to this point, cooled, covered and refrigerated for up to 2 days. Bring to a simmer before continuing.
2. Add zucchini cut in chunks and chicken; cover and simmer for 10 minutes, or until chicken is no longer pink inside and vegetables are tender. Add parsley; season with salt and pepper to taste. Cook couscous according to package directions. 6 servings

---

[71]https://www.bing.com/search?q=Moroccan+Chicken+Stew&filters=

Ryan's Favorite beef   Jennifer Hegyi

Ingredients

1 jar 128 ml vegetable beef and spaghetti
1 banana

Ryan's Favorite beef[72]

Instructions

1. Remove half of vegetable beet and spaghetti from jar, place it on a plate, heat it in microwave for 10-15 seconds.
2. Peer banana, cut in half and mash finely. Put banana beside beef and Ryan (9 month old) is already pounding the table for it!

---

[72] https://www.bing.com/search?q=Ryane

Recipes of Canadian Martyrs and St. Margaret Mary Church

Fish

Mary Dalipaj

Corry Wink

Recipes of Canadian Martyrs and St. Margaret Mary Church

Fisherman's delight (halaszle)   Frank Hegyi

Ingredients

2 x 800 g whole perch, filleted, (bones and heads reserved
3 tomatoes, peeled, finely chopped
2 tbsp Hungarian sweet paprika
3 flat leaved parsley
2 tbsp sour cream
60 ml (¼ cup) olive oil
2 onions, finely chopped

Fisherman's delight (halaszle)

Instructions

1. Cut fish into 3 cm pieces and refrigerate. Heat 1 tbsp oil over medium-low heat, add fish heads and bones and cook, turning once, for 2 minutes.
2. Add 3 litres cold water. Bring to a simmer and cook for 30 minutes. Strain through a fine sieve lined with muslin, discarding solids.
3. Heat oil in a large saucepan over medium heat. Add onions and capsicum, and cook, stirring, for 4 minutes or until softened. Add tomatoes and cook, stirring occasionally, for a further 5 minutes. Add paprika and stir for 1 minute or until fragrant, then return strained stock to the pan.
4. Simmer for 40 minutes and season with salt and pepper.
5. Add fish pieces and simmer for 10 minutes or until just cooked. Season again.

Baked Salmon
Frank Hegyi

Ingredients

1 whole salmon about 8-10 lbs
2 bunches green onions chopped
1 lemon, cut into slices
1 bunch fresh dill, chopped up
2 onions, sliced

2 tsp salt
2 tsp pepper
1 tsp paprika
½ lb butter

Baked Salmon

Instructions

1. Clean salmon on the outside by removing scales and wipe inside with wet paper towel. On large tin foil (may put 3 pieces of rolls 12"x18"), place salmon in dish.
2. Place inside and outside salmon sliced onions and half of dill. Place lemon, butter, rest of dill and chopped onion inside the fish.
3. Wrap fish in tin foil. Bake fish in oven at 350 F for 30 minutes or until salmon is cooked but moist inside. It can also be cooked on the BBQ. Serve with Potato slices and tossed salad.

Mustard salmon Frank Hegyi

Ingredients

4 salmon steaks
2 tbsp wholegrain mustard
1 tsp salt

10 mushrooms
1 packet sour cream
1 tsp black pepper

Mustard Salmon[73]

Instructions

1. Wash and dry the salmon. Season with salt and pepper.
2. Arrange in an ovenproof dish with the sliced mushrooms.
3. Mix mustard with the cream and pour over salmon and mushrooms.
4. Cook in a preheated 350 F oven for about 20 minutes. Serve with boiled potatoes and a salad.

---

[73] http://allrecipes.com/recipe/220692/salmon-with-mustard-cream-sauce/

Quick Shrimp and Corn Chowder   Pamela DiNardo

Ingredients

Cooking Spray
1 cup chopped green bell pepper
¾ cup cream cheese softened
1 can cream style corn
1 can condensed cream of mushroom
1 ¼ lb medium or small shrimp, peeled, tails off and deveined
1 cup chopped onion
1 garlic clove minced
2 cups milk
1 can diced tomatoes
4 tsp green onions

Shrimp and Corn Chowder[74]

Instructions

1. Heat Dutch oven or large saucepan coated with cooking spray over medium high heat.
2. Add chopped onion, bell pepper and garlic. Sauté 5 minutes.
3. Stir in cream cheese, reduce heat and cook until cheese melts.
4. Add milk and next 3 ingredients, cook 10 minutes stirring occasionally. Bring milk mixture to a boil.
5. Add shrimp, cook 5 minutes or until shrimp are done. Remove from heat. Sprinkle each serving with green onions.

---

[74] http://allrecipes.com/recipe/86096/grandmas-corn-chowde

Sweet Potato Chili Casserole   Lorna Kingston

Ingredients

1 or 2 Italian sausages   2 onions, chopped
3   minced garlic cloves   1 tsp of oregano
4   medium-sized sweet potatoes, peeled and diced
1 tsp of cumin
8 oz can of diced tomatoes   1/2 tsp of sugar
1/4 tsp of salt   1 teaspoon to 1 tablespoon of chili powder
19 oz can of red kidney or black beans, drained and rinsed

Sweet Potato Chili Casserole

Instructions

1. Remove sausages from their casings and brown.
2. Stir onions and garlic, chili powder, oregano and cumin into sausages.
3. Stir until fragrant (about 2 minutes).
4. Add tomatoes, including juice, beans and diced sweet potatoes.
5. Bring to a boil. Then reduce heat to low so the mixture simmers, covered, until potatoes are tender (about 30 minutes). Taste, and if needed, stir in sugar and salt. Serve sprinkled with freshly chopped coriander or parsley.

Low Carb Sausage and pepperoni pizza stuffed Red peppers   Nancy MacDonald

Ingredients
1 pkg. (19.5 oz) Italian sausage or turkey Italian sausage links, uncooked
1 small onion, chopped
2-3 tsp. olive oil
1 tsp minced garlic
1 jar pizza sauce, 14 oz.
2 tsp dried oregano
3 large bell peppers, cut in half lengthwise and stem and seeds removed
3 oz. pepperoni, 12 pieces cut in half for the top of the peppers and the rest chopped
2 cups + 1/2 cup grated Mozzarella cheese

Low Carb Sausage[75]

Instructions
1. First let's make the stuffing mixture.
2. Heat a little olive oil in a large frying pan and brown the sausage well, breaking apart as it cooks. (I use a potato masher to break apart the meat; don't laugh!) When sausage is brown, push it over to cook the onions and garlic.
3. Then add the pizza sauce and simmer until the sauce has cooked down a lot; the mixture should be barely wet. (Look for the lowest-sugar sauce you can find. For me this was Ragu Homemade Style Pizza Sauce which only adds 5 carbs per serving to this dish. Turn off the heat and stir in the chopped pepperoni and grated cheese.
4. Cut the pepper in half lengthwise, cutting away the stem but trying to leave the end part to help hold in the filling. Divide the pizza stuffing mixture between the six pepper halves and bake in a preheated 375F/190C oven for 20 minutes.
5. Remove from oven and put grated Mozzarella and pepperoni halves on top of each pepper. Bake about 25 minutes more, or until cheese is nicely melted and browned.

---

[75] http://bitesofflavor.com/wp-content/uploads/2017/05/Turkey-Pizza-Stuffed-Peppers.jpg

Mussels Provençale   Pamela DiNardo

Ingredients

48 Fresh Atlantic Mussels scrubbed debearded
3 cloves garlic, finely chopped
2 stalks celery, chopped
3 ½ cups canned tomatoes drained
½ cup chopped fresh basil or 1 tsp dry basil

½ cup vegetable oil and
3 medium onions, chopped
1 cup tomato paste
2 cups dry white wine
Salt and pepper to taste

Mussels Provençale[76]

Instructions

1. Sauté garlic in hot oil in heavy sauce pan, add onion and celery; cook until soft but not brown.
2. Add tomatoes; simmer 10 min, to evaporate remaining liquid. Add remaining ingredients except mussels, simmer 30 min. Before serving, add mussels, cover, simmer 3-5 minutes or until mussels are open. Don't eat any that have not opened.
3. You can make the sauce ahead of time, and then just steam the mussels with either water or white wine and then mix the two together. If you want to have it a bit runnier to dip bread in the tomato sauce, don't drain the can of tomatoes.

---

[76] http://allrecipes.com/recipe/50708/mussels-provencal/

Seafood pasta   Frank Hegyi

Ingredients

½ lb shrimp
2 garlic cloves, chopped
3 tbsp of soft cheese
1 small jar of tomato sauce
1 tsp salt
1 tsp chopped parsley

½ lb salmon
5 mushrooms
1 tbsp oil
1 pkg macaroni
1 tsp pepper

Seafood Pasta[77]

Instructions

1. Heat the oil in a pan, add the chopped garlic and cook for a minute, add the shrimp and fish (cut in small pieces), season with salt and pepper.
2. In 2-3 minutes, add the mushrooms (chopped finely), cook for a further minute, add the soft cheese, when the cheese has melted into a creamy sauce add the tomato sauce.
3. Cook for a further 5 minutes. Sprinkle the parsley. Cook macaroni according to instructions on package.

---

[77] http://allrecipes.com/recipes/410/main-dish/pasta/seafood/

Smoked Salmon Spirals   Pamela DiNardo

Ingredients

1 pkg of smoked salmon (350 g)   1/3 cup red onion, minced
1 pkg of crepes (or make your own)   1 tbsp capers, minced
1 container of spreadable cream cheese (250g)

Smoked Salmon Spirals[78]

Instructions

1. In a medium-sized bowl, combine the cream cheese, red onions and capers. Mix well. Lay one crepe on a dry work surface and spread with 2 tbsp of the cream cheese mixture.
2. Top with a slice of smoked salmon and roll up tightly. Set to one side and repeat procedure with remaining crepes.
3. Cover with plastic wrap and refrigerate. When ready to serve, unwrap crepes and cut on an angle into pieces, about 1 ½" thick.
4. Serve with a garnish of capers, lemon slices and baby greens.

---

[78] http://www.geniuskitchen.com/recipe/smoked-salmon-spirals-402190

Baked Fish   Maureen Cerroni

Ingredients

2 lbs fish fillets
1/2 cup mayonnaise
1/2 tsp dry mustard
Black pepper taste

1 tsp minced onion
1/2 tsp marjoram
1 tsp lemon juice
Paprika

Baked Fish[79]

Instructions

1. Preheat oven to 400°F.
2. Place fish in oiled baking dish.
3. Mix remaining ingredients except paprika. Spread over fish.
4. Bake for 20 minutes until browned.
5. Sprinkle with paprika.

---

[79] http://2.bp.blogspot.com/-TcWhEI2RAk/TeLJR6N4KGI/Lw/AIsijw0cEl0/s1600/Baked+Fish+Fillet2.jpg

Recipes of Canadian Martyrs and St. Margaret Mary Church

Tuna Twirl Surprise

Anne Louise Mahoney

Ingredients

- 1 tsp. oil
- 1 medium onion, chopped
- ⅔ cup water
- 1 (284 ml). can of cream of celery soup, undiluted
- 2 cups hot cooked rotini
- 1 tsp. curry powder
- 1 tsp. curry powder
- ¼ tsp. Pepper
- 1 (170 gram) can of tuna, drained
- ½ cups frozen green peas

Tuna Twirl Surprise[80]

Instructions

1. Heat oil in large skillet; add onion and sauté until tender. Combine water, curry powder, pepper and soup in a bowl.
2. Stir well and pour into skillet.
3. Add rotini, peas, and tuna; stir well.
4. Cook uncovered, over low heat for 10 minutes, stirring occasionally. 4 servings

---

[80]https://www.bing.com/images/search?q=tuna+twirl+surprise&id

Recipes of Canadian Martyrs and St. Margaret Mary Church

Crab Foo Yung   Mary Poulin

Ingredients

4 Eggs, Beaten
⅓ cup green onions, sliced
½ lb. cooked crab, small
⅛ tsp. garlic powder
½ tsp. salt
2 tbsp foo yung sauce
1 tsp. sugar
½ cup chicken broth

½ lb. bean sprouts
6 mushrooms, sliced
½ lb shrimp
1/8 tsp. pepper
2 tbsp. salad oil
1 ½tsp. cornstarch
2 tsp. soy sauce
1 tsp. vinegar

Crab Foo Yung[81]

Instructions

1. Combine eggs, bean sprouts, onion, crab and seasoning. Heat wok or fry pan over medium-high heat. When hot, add oil.
2. Add 1/4 cup of egg mixture for each patty. Fry, turning once when lightly browned and cooked to your liking, about 2 minutes per side.
3. Continue with remaining batter, adding more oil if needed. Meanwhile make sauce. Place wok over low heat. When hot add all ingredients. Stir until thickened.

---

[81] https://www.bing.com/search?q=Crab+Foo+Yung&filters=

Shrimp Basil
Mike MacNeil

Ingredients

¼ c butter or margarine
2 tbsp green pepper, finely chopped
1 cup sliced mushrooms
¼ tsp pepper
½ tsp salt
4 tbsp dry white wine
¼ c sour cream

½ cup chopped celery
1 ¾ tsp basil
2 ½ tbsp cornstarch
½ c chicken broth
¼ c evaporated milk
1 tbsp ketchup

Shrimp Basil[82]

Instructions

1. 400 g frozen shrimp
2. Cook vegetables in butter until onion is transparent.
3. Blend in flour mixture, then liquids. Cook until thickened. Gently stir in shrimp. Heat. At last minute stir in sour cream. Do not boil. Serve over pasta, garnished.

---

[82] https://www.bing.com/search?q=Basil+Shrimp&filters=ufn%3a%22Basil+Shrimp

Tuna Macaroni Casserole Mary Poulin

Ingredients

1 can cream of mushroom soup
1 7oz dm tuna, drained, flaked
2 cups cooked macaroni
½ cup additional cheddar

½ cup milk
¼ cup chopped onion
½ cup cheddar cheese
2 tbsp. bread crumbs

Tuna Macaroni Casserole[83]

Instructions

1. In a buttered casserole dish, blend soup, milk, tuna, onion, cooked macaroni and the first 1/2 cup shredded cheddar.
2. Sprinkle top with second 1/2 cup of cheese. Cover and refrigerate.
3. Remove 30 minutes before serving. Top with buttered bread crumbs (may uses snack cracker crumbs); bake at 400 F. for about 30 minutes or until bubbly.

---

[83] https://www.bing.com/search?q=Tuna+Macaroni+Casserole&filters=ufn%3a%22Tuna+Macaroni+Casserole

Salmon Quiche — Joanne Robichaud

Ingredients

- 1 1-2 cup rice
- 2 cup water
- 2 tbsp butter
- 1 chicken bouillon cube
- 1 salmon fillet (6 to 8 ounces) or 1 can of salmon
- 2 tsp dried red bell pepper
- 1 tsp lemon zest
- 3 or 4 eggs
- 2 tbsp chopped parsley
- 1 cup grated Swiss or cheddar cheese
- 1-4 cup chopped green onion
- ¼ tsp salt
- 1 cup liquid (salmon juice with milk)
- few drops of Tabasco
- ¼ cup sliced almonds

Salmon Quiche[84]

Instructions

1. Cook rice with water, butter and chicken bouillon.
2. When cooked, cool and add chopped parsley.
3. Put rice mixture in the bottom of a 10 inch diameter buttered pie plate and mould to the plate.
4. Cover with the grated cheese and the green onion. Put uncooked salmon or canned salmon in big chunks over the rice mixture.
5. Mix bell pepper, lemon zest, eggs, salmon juice with milk, salt and Tabasco and pour over the salmon. Cook at 350 F for half an hour. Put sliced almonds on top of quiche and continue cooking until the top of the quiche is firm.

---

[84]https://www.bing.com/search?q=Crustless+Salmon+Quiche&filters=ufn%3a%22Crustless+Salmon+Quiche%22

Vegetarian and Pasta

Mike Charrier

Terri White Lobsinger

Cathrinne Clifford

Cabbage Rolls Holubtsi Rose Hegyi

Ingredients

1 medium sized cabbage
2 cups rice
1 onion finely chopped
¼ cup margarine for rice
1 rib celery, finely choppe

1 tbsp salt
1 tsp pepper
1 can tomato soup
¼ cup margarine

Cabbage Rolls Holubtsi

Instructions

1. Cook rice in water slightly underdone. Mix in margarine.
2. Sauté onions and celery in margarine and add to the rice and stir.
3. Cook bacon until crisp, cut into small pieces and add to rice (this is optional and should be omitted for vegetarian option). Mix well.
4. Remove core from cabbage. Place cabbage in pot with boiling water covering to top. Simmer cabbage long enough until leaves wilt. Remove cabbage from pot then separate leaves. Remove the hard centre part of the leaves. Cut leaves in half if large. Prepare roast pan by placing outer cabbage leaves on the bottom. On each cabbage piece, held in the palm, put a spoonful of rice mixture, roll up lightly and place into roast pan.
5. Complete this until all cabbage leaves are used up. Heat up tomato soup and pour it into roast pan. Add margarine and cover it with outer cabbage leaves or the hard centre parts previously removed. Cover roast pan with lid and place in over at 350 F and cook for 1-1½ hours until tender.

Vegetarian Lecsó Frank Hegyi

Ingredients

1 onions, cut into cubes
2 green peppers
2 red pepper
1 tomatoes, sliced into cubes
2 oz vegetable oil

2 tsp salt
1 tsp dill
1 tsp ginger
1 tsp ground pepper

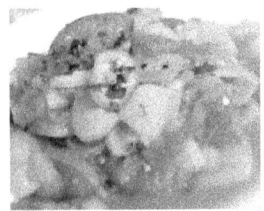

Lecsó[85]

Instructions

1. Warm oil in a pot on medium heat. Put in chopped up onions and sauté until tender. Put in green peppers, cut in strips, red peppers, cut in strips and tomato and cook under medium heat for 30 minutes, pouring in enough water to make sure that the mixture does not stick to the bottom of the pot.
2. Season with salt, pepper, dill and ginger. Cook for another 15 minutes or until mixture is tender

---

[85] http://lecsgyorsetterem.hu/a-lecsorol/

Recipes of Canadian Martyrs and St. Margaret Mary Church

Hungarian Nokedli

Jennifer Hegyi

Ingredients

3 eggs
2 oz vegetable oil
4 cups flour
2 cups milk

1 tsp salt for mixture
2 tsp salt for water
½ lb butter

Nokedli[86]

Instructions

1. Mix eggs, oil, milk and salt in a bowl. Add water or a little more flour until dough is smooth but not too thick. Let it stand for 10 minutes. Fill large pot with water up to 2 inches away from top. Bring water to boil and add salt.
2. Place Spaetzel make on the large pan, fill with dough and place it top the boiling water and sieve it in. Let it boil for 2-3 minutes until dough rises to the top of water. Place large sieve in the plastic bowl, use small sieve to remove the cooked dough from the pan into the large sieve, put it under the running water from sink just to remove the starch, then empty it into the Pyrex dish.
3. Put some of the butter or margarine on top of it, cover with lid and put into oven under low heat. Repeat this process until all dough is used up.

---

[86] http://www.geniuskitchen.com/recipe/hungarian-nokedli-dumplings-54823

Recipes of Canadian Martyrs and St. Margaret Mary Church

Noodles and rice with peas Evelyn Kelly

Ingredients

2 tbsp butter
1 ½ cups long grain rice
3 cups frozen peas
Salt and pepper to taste

1 ½ cups of broken fine egg noodles
4 cups chicken stock (broth)
¾ cup chopped fresh dill

Noodles and rice with peas[87]

Instructions

1 In a heavy saucepan, melt butter; add noodles and cook over medium heat, stirring constantly for about 6 minutes. Be careful not to burn the butter; lower heat as needed.
2 Add rice and stir-cook for 1 minute.
3 Pour in stock; bring to a boil, cover, and simmer gently for about 20 minutes or until liquid is absorbed completely.
4 Stir in peas (still frozen) dill, salt, and pepper. If serving immediately, simmer for 5 minutes or until peas are heated through.
5 If serving later: transfer to a large casserole, cover and refrigerate for up to 2 days.
6 To reheat, pour in ½ cup of boiling stock (or water); cover and place in 375 degree oven for about 20 minutes until heated through. Fluff gently with a fork and serve.

---

[87]https://www.vegetariantimes.com/.image/c_limit

Spaghetti Carbonara   Rosemary O'Connell

Ingredients

1 lb spaghetti
2 cloves minced
1 cup grated parmesan cheese
6 or 8-pieces pancetta or bacon chopped
3 eggs at room temperature (important to achieve a creamy texture)
Freshly ground black pepper

Spaghetti Carbonara[88]

Instructions

1. Whisk grated parmesan cheese, room temperature eggs & black pepper in a bowl.
2. Cook chopped pancetta or bacon on medium heat till crispy. Remove from heat. In same pan, cook garlic for 1 min.
3. Cook the spaghetti (al dente) in salted water according to package directions.
4. Drain, reserving 1 cup of pasta water.
5. Toss the hot (also important) spaghetti in with the pancetta/garlic mixture & toss to coat. Quickly add the sauce to the hot pasta and toss to combine. The hot pasta will thicken the eggs.
6. Add the pasta water to adjust consistency.

This is a quick dinner ready in 1/2 hr. Can serve 6 or have some leftovers

---

[88]https://www.seriouseats.com/images/2017/02/20170210-vegan-carbonara-spaghetti-vicky-wasik-12.jpg

Horseradish Smashed Potatoes — Pamela DiNardo

Ingredients

12 large Yukon Gold potatoes, unpeeled, washed and cut into quarters
1 cup of milk
2 tsp prepared horseradish
1 stick of butter
Salt and pepper to taste

Horseradish Smashed Potatoes[89]

Instructions

1. Boil potatoes for 15 – 20 minutes until tender when pierced with a knife
2. Meanwhile heat the milk, butter and horseradish in a small pot
3. Place potatoes in a bowl and pour hot milk mixture over them, smash well and season with salt and pepper

---

[89] http://allrecipes.com/recipe/22658/mashed-potatoes-with-horseradish/

Recipes of Canadian Martyrs and St. Margaret Mary Church

Oma Trudi's Dough Andress Dumplings
(Mehlkloesse / Mehlköβe)   Pamela Dixon

Ingredients

500 g flour
30 g Yeast
40 g white sugar
½ tsp salt
250 mL milk, warmed
2 eggs
2 tbsp butter

Steaming sauce ingredients – for each pot used:
200 mL milk   2 tbsp butter
50 g sugar

Serving ingredients
Sour cherry sauce or fruit compote or jam or jelly

Dough Andress Dumplings[90]

Instructions

1. Put the flour into a bowl. If using quick rise yeast, add the yeast to the flour. If using regular yeast, add to the warmed milk with the sugar – let sit for a few minutes to ensure yeast bloom. Add the warmed milk/yeast mixture to the flour. Add the eggs, butter and salt. Mix until a smooth dough forms. The dough should be very soft – that is what you are looking for! Place in a warm spot and let rise for 30 minutes.

---

[90] https://i.dailymail.co.uk/i/pix/

Recipes of Canadian Martyrs and St. Margaret Mary Church

2. After 30 minutes, transfer dough to a floured surface. You want to make 12 balls. The dough may be very sticky. That is fine – use some extra flour on your hands and on the dough to help manipulate it. I normally make a 2 inch roll of dough and then cut out twelve segments that I roll into balls. You could do balls by weight or any other method you are familiar with.
3. Once the balls are made, cover and let rise for 25 minutes. I don't think you need to transfer the balls to let them rise, you could leave them on the floured surface and just put a tea towel on top while prepping the rest. The balls should increase in size during this resting period.
4. The dumplings will be steamed in a milk mixture on the stove. You will need a pot with walls at least four inches. You could use more than one pot depending on how big your pot is and if all the dumplings will fit in it. Add the milk, butter and sugar to the pot and heat up. The liquid should be gently bubbling but not boiling. Add balls/dumplings to the pot, cover and let cook on medium heat. You want the liquid to reduce and the sugar to begin caramelizing so the bottoms of the dumplings begin to brown, usually 20-25 minutes depending on your temperature.
5. You can check the progress, but if you remove the lid, the heat escapes and it may take a bit of time for the contents to get back to medium high heat again. Try to be patient; but if you smell burning – check the dumplings!
6. To test if ready, take 2 forks and open the top of one of the dumplings. The inside should look dry like a sponge and not gummy.
7. When done, add a dab of butter to the dumpling. A serving is one or two dumplings.
8. Our family enjoys these dumplings with a heated sour cherry sauce; however. they could be good with any fruit compote/sauce or jam or jelly.

When I have had some over browned dumplings, I remove from the heat and let cool a bit. When removing from the pan, the burnt bottom may come off and stick in the pan – the remainder should be fine. If the whole dumpling comes out, cut off the burnt bit and serve with the bottom up – lathered in butter and fruit sauce.

Recipes of Canadian Martyrs and St. Margaret Mary Church

Individual Plum Tarts — Margaret Moriarty

Ingredients

Tart shells
2 tsp sugar   1/2 tsp ground cinnamon
1 (17.33-oz) package (2 sheets) frozen puff pastry sheets, thawed
2 tsp Land O Lakes® Butter, melted
Plum filling
1/4 cup Butter   1/4 cup sugar
6 medium (4 cups) red plums, sliced, pitted
1/2 tsp ground cinnamon
Cream filling
1/2 cup powdered sugar   2 tbsp milk
1 (8-ounce) package cream cheese, softened
1 tsp vanilla

Individual Plum Tarts[91]

Instructions

1. Heat oven to 350°F
2. Combine 2 tablespoons sugar and 1/2 teaspoon cinnamon in small bowl; set aside.
3. Cut each sheet of puff pastry into 4 (5-inch) squares on lightly floured surface. Fold each square in half diagonally forming a triangle. Starting at folded side cut 1/2-inch border strip on both sides of triangle leaving 3/4-inch uncut at point so strips remain attached. Unfold triangle. Lift both cut border strips and pull one under the other, pulling to match corners on base.

---

[91] http://www.simplyrecipes.com/wp-content/uploads/2005/06/plum-cobbler.jpg

Recipes of Canadian Martyrs and St. Margaret Mary Church

4. Brush with 2 tablespoons melted butter; sprinkle with sugar mixture. Prick all over center of each square with fork. Place onto 2 ungreased baking sheets. Bake 25-30 minutes or until golden brown. Cool completely.
5. Meanwhile, place all plum filling ingredients in 10-inch skillet. Cook over medium heat, stirring occasionally, 5-8 minutes or until plums are tender and juice is slightly thickened. Cool to room temperature.
6. Combine all cream filling ingredients in small bowl. Beat at medium speed, scraping bowl often, until smooth.
7. To serve, place each baked tart shell onto individual dessert plate. Spread bottom of each tart shell with about 2 tablespoons cream filling. Divide plums among tarts; drizzle with plum filling liquid.
8. These tarts are delicious though they take a long time to prepare

Bud Hendley's Spaghetti Sauce

Marion Lochnan and Rosemarie Hoey

Ingredients

3 lb lean ground beef
28 oz can diced tomatoes
5 ½ oz tomato paste
1 tsp onion powder
1 tsp cayenne pepper
1 tsp oregano
1 tsp marjoram
1 tsp thyme
6 drops hot pepper sauce
Salt and pepper to taste

1 bottle spiced sauce (Farm Boy)
4 oz tomato sauce
1 tsp garlic powder
1 tsp basil
1 tsp Italian seasoning
1 tsp paprika
1 tsp sage
1 tsp chillies, crushed
2 or 3 garlic buds, chopped

Spaghetti Sauce[92]

Instructions

1. Brown ground beef.
2. With potato masher, try to mash the ground beef very fine after browning.
3. Then add all the ingredients.
4. Simmer for 2 hours.
5. Serve with pasta. Freezes well.

---

[92] https://ohsweetbasil.com/wp-content/uploads/The-secret-to-authentic-spaghetti-sauce-ohsweetbasil.com-6.jpg

Ben's Lasagna Fr. Tim Coonen

Ingredients:

Sauce:
1 28-oz can crushed tomatoes   1 15-oz can tomato sauce
1 15-oz can diced tomatoes   ½ lb ground beef
½ lb Italian sausage links, diced   3 tbsp onion, diced
1 tsp garlic, minced   ½ tsp granulated garlic
1 tsp basil   1 tsp oregano
½ tsp crushed red pepper flakes   1 tsp parsley flakes
salt to taste   white pepper to taste
2 tsp sugar   3 tsp grated Parmesan cheese
Cheese Filling:
15 oz Ricotta cheese   16 oz cottage cheese
1 egg yolk   salt and black pepper to taste
Other Ingredients:
1/2 lb (10) lasagna noodles cooked per directions on box.
36 pepperoni slices (I use more if I have them...)
14 oz mozzarella cheese, shredded   1 cup Parmesan cheese, grated

Ben's Lasagna[93]

Instructions

1. In a large, heavy pan brown the ground beef, sausage, onion, and garlic. Drain.
2. Cook 5 more minutes.
3. Add the rest of the ingredients and heat slowly.
4. Simmer for 2 hours stirring frequently.

---

[93] https://cdn3.tmbi.com/secure/RMS/attachments/37/1200x1200/Best-Lasagna_exps3.

Recipes of Canadian Martyrs and St. Margaret Mary Church

5. When sauce is done put a light layer of sauce on the bottom of a 9 x 13 inch baking dish.
6. Lay 5 lasagna noodles on bottom of pan, overlapping slightly.
7. Spread half of the cheese filling on top of the noodles.
8. Spread half of the meat sauce on top of the cheese filling.
9. Layer half of the pepperoni over the meat sauce.
10. Sprinkle half of the Parmesan and half of the mozzarella over the pepperoni.
11. Repeat all layers.
12. Bake in oven at 350°F for 30 to 45 minutes until the cheese is golden brown.
13. Tip: In the middle use more sauce and less cheese, and on top use more cheese and less sauce. Otherwise you just get noodles pressed together.

A few years ago, I dropped into my sister's place. Surprise: her 15-year-old son was making supper. Bigger surprise: his killer lasagna was terrific. I've served it to our parish council and had to email everybody the recipe. The secret: pepperoni, found in the deli section, pre-sliced for pizza toppings.

Brussels Sprouts — Fr. Tim Coonen

Ingredients:

1 lb Brussels sprouts (trimmed and cleaned)
3 tbsp honey   1 ½ tbsp olive oil

Brussels Sprouts[94]

Instructions

1. Cut sprouts in half and tear off outer leaf set.
2. Toss all ingredients in a bowl, then place on a sheet pan.
3. Bake in the oven at 350 degrees for 30 minutes (with the convection blower off, if you have a convection oven)
4. Turn blower on (or broiler on low) and bake for another 5-10 minutes, until the honey begins to caramelize.

Serves 4-6.
Delicious Brussels Sprouts are possible! This is from the Duluth Grill's first cookbook, and it's one of their most-asked-for recipes. P

---

[94] http://assets.simplyrecipes.com/wp-content/uploads/2013/02/20153559/hoisin-glazed-brussels-sprouts-vertical-b-1800.jpg

Crepes
Pamela DiNardo

Ingredients

1 cup flour
2 eggs
½ cup milk

½ cup water
2 tbsp butter melted
¼ tsp salt

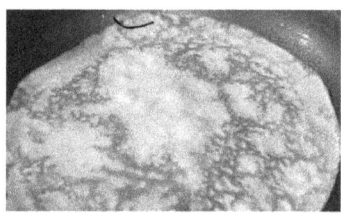

Crepes[95]

Instructions

1. In a large mixing bowl, whisk together the flour and the eggs. Gradually add in the milk and water, stirring to combine. Add the salt and butter beat until smooth.
2. Heat a lightly oiled griddle or frying pan over medium high heat. Pour or scoop the batter onto the griddle using approximately ¼ cup for each crepe. Tilt the pan with a circular motion so that the batter coats the surface evenly.
3. Cook the crepe for about 2 minutes until the bottom is light brown. Loosen with a spatula, turn and cook the other side. Serve hot

---

[95] http://allrecipes.com/recipe/16383/basic-crepes/

Scalloped Potatoes
Pamela DiNardo

Ingredients

2 tbsp butter
2 tbsp flour
2 ½ cup milk   Pinch of nutmeg
4 oz herbed cream cheese
¾ cup grated Swiss cheese

½ tsp salt
¼ tsp pepper
5 medium potatoes
¼ cup parmesan cheese

Scalloped Potatoes[96]

Instructions

1. Melt butter in medium saucepan. Wisk in flour. Cook 2 – 3 minutes without browning, stirring constantly. Wisk in milk. Bring to a boil. Reduce heat, simmer for 5 minutes.
2. Add herbed cheese, Swiss cheese, salt, pepper and nutmeg. Stir until cheese melts.
3. Meanwhile slice potatoes in ¼" slices, layer potatoes and sauce ending with sauce. Sprinkle with parmesan
4. Bake in preheated oven at 350 for 1 hour and 2o minutes until potatoes are tender.
5. Let stand 5 – 10 minutes before serving

---

[96] http://allrecipes.com/recipe/16455/easy-scalloped-potatoes

Baked Pasta Florentine — Pamela DiNardo

Ingredients

20 oz frozen chopped spinach
3 cups cooked spiral pasta
1 ½ cups shredded Cheddar cheese
1 can cream mushrooms or celery soup
1 grated peel & juice of one lemon
Cook well and drain spinach

3 slightly beaten eggs
¼ cup finely chopped onion
½ tsp of celery salt
¼ tsp pepper

Baked Pasta Florentine[97]

Instructions

1. Combine with pasta and add rest of ingredients.
2. Pour into shallow baking dish. Bake at 350 for 30 minutes.
3. Top with extra cheese if desired.

---

[97] http://www.kraftrecipes.com/recipes/dinner/baked-pasta-casseroles.aspx

Cheese Shells — Pamela DiNardo

Ingredients

Filings. 1 cups cottage cheese
1 egg slightly beaten
1 tbsp parsley minced
4 tbsp parmesan
Chopped onion
2 stalks celery finely chopped
Sauce. ¼ lb butter
1 cup heavy cream
¼ tsp tobasco sauce
2 cups Monterey Jack cheese

1 tsp basil
¼ tsp nutmeg
½ tsp salt
¼ tsp ground pepper
2 carrots finely chopped]

7 tbsp flour
3 cups chicken broth
Salt to taste

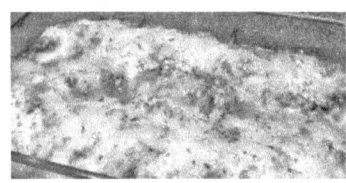

Cheese Shells[98]

Instructions

1. Sauté onions, celery and carrots mix with remaining ingredients.
2. Melt butter, stir in flour, cook for 3 minutes. Stir in broth and cream and cook for another 3 minutes until smooth and thick. Add cheese, tobasco and salt.
3. Cook until the cheese melts
4. Fill shells and arrange in casserole dish.
5. Pour sauce over filled shells and bake in 350 oven for 20 minutes.

---

[98] http://allrecipes.com/recipe/21532/stuffed-shells-iii/

Greek Pasta Salad
Pamela DiNardo

Ingredients

1½ cups penne pasta
1 up crumbled feta cheese
1/3 cup sliced black olives
½ medium sweet green pepper, sliced
1 cup diced cucumber
2 large tomatoes, diced
2 green onions, chopped
¼ cup finely chopped fresh mint

Dressing

2 tbsp olive oil
2 tbsp cider vinegar
1.2 tsp dried oregano leaves
1 clove garlic, minced
1 tsp sugar and lemon juice
¼ tsp pepper

Greek Pasta Salad[99]

Instructions

1. In a large pot of boiling water, cook pasta according to package directions, drain and rinse under cold water. Drain again.
2. In a large bowl combine pasta, feta cheese, cucumber, tomatoes, olives, green pepper and mint
3. Mix
4. Mix dressing ingredients and pour over top.
5. Mix and serve.

---

[99] http://allrecipes.com/recipe/176650/greek-pasta-salad/

Yummy carrot cake with cream cheese icing

Josie Mousseau

Ingredients

2 cups grated raw carrots
1 cup golden raisins
1 cup white sugar
4 eggs beaten
1 cup whole wheat flour
½ tsp baking powder
1 tsp salt

1 ½ cup peeled grated apples
½ cup chopped walnuts or pecans:
1 cup vegetable oil
1 cup all-purpose flour
1 ½ tsp baking soda
2 tsp cinnamon

Yummy carrot cake with cream cheese icing[100]

Instructions

1. Place all ingredients in a bowl to be ready to be added to the batter once step 3 is completed
2. Combine all wet ingredients in bowl and beat on medium setting of mixer until thickened (approx. 4 minutes)
3. Place all dry ingredients in a bowl, then combine with the wet ingredients from step 2 until lightly combined, do not overmix. Add ingredients from step #1, mix until combined.
4. Place mixture in a greased bundt pan. Bake at 350ºF oven for 45-55 minutes (varies based on accuracy of your oven temperature). Let cool for 5 minutes removing from bundt pan and at least one hour before icing.

Ingredients for icing

---

[100] https://cookiescakespiesohmy.files.wordpress.com/2013/06/carrot-cake-with-cream-cheese-frosting.jpg

5. 1/4 cup butter – room temperature (Dash of salt if using unsalted butter)
6. ½ package cream cheese – room temperature
7. 1 tsp vanilla
8. 1 ½ cup icing sugar – sifted
9. 1 tsp milk

Directions for icing

10. cream butter, then add cream cheese and beat on medium until fluffy (4-5 minutes). Add salt and vanilla, beat until combined.
11. Add icing sugar, with mixer on low until combined then increase speed to medium and beat for another 4-5 minutes.
12. Add milk to desired consistency of preference for icing. Icing can be placed on the cake as desired (piping onto cake makes a lovely presentation).
13. Cake can be made 1-2 days in advance of icing.
14. Yield: 12-14 pieces

Recipes of Canadian Martyrs and St. Margaret Mary Church

Chicken Curry with Red Peppers and Coconut Milk
Fran Banks

Ingredients

1 1/2 lb (675 g) skinless, boneless chicken breast, cut into cubes
1 large onion cut into 10 wedges   2 tbsp (30 ml) olive oil
1 red bell pepper, cut into squares   2 cloves garlic chopped finely
2 cloves garlic chopped finely   2 tsp (10 ml) chili powder
2 tsp (10 ml) curry powder   1 tbsp (15 ml) honey
1/2 tsp (2.5 ml) ground turmeric   1 can (398 ml/14 oz) coconut milk
salt and pepper

Chicken Curry[101]

Preparation
1. In a large skillet over high heat, sauté the onion and bell pepper in the oil until soft and gold-coloured. Add the chicken, garlic, and spices. Sauté for about 2 minutes. Season with salt and pepper.
2. Add the coconut milk and honey. Bring to a boil, reduce the heat and simmer gently until the chicken is cooked through, about 8 minutes. Adjust the seasoning.

Preparation 10 min; Cooking 15 min; Servings 4

---

[101] https://www.bing.com/search?q=Chicken+Curry&filters -

Penne, Prosciutto and Peas Pamela DiNardo

Ingredients

4 cups Penne Rigate
10 slices prosciutto, cut into thin slices
½ lb peas, cooked
¼ chopped onion
2 cups heavy whipping cream

2 tbsp butter
2 tsp cornstarch
½ cup minced fresh parsley
150 g shredded parmesan

Penne, Prosciutto and Peas[102]

Instructions

1. Cook pasta according to package directions.
2. Meanwhile, in a large skillet sauté the peas and onion in butter until tender. Add prosciutto, sauté for 3 minutes.
3. In a bowl, combine the cornstarch, cream and two tablespoons of Parmigiano Reggiano until smooth, stir into the skillet. Add parsley and pepper.
4. Bring to a boil, cook and stir for 2 minutes or until thickened. Drain pasta, add to the skillet and stir to coat. Sprinkle with Parmesan.

---

[102] http://allrecipes.com/recipe/87433/pasta-and-peas

Fresh Pasta　　　　　　　　　　　　　　Pamela DiNardo

Ingredients

3 eggs　　　　　　　　　　　　　　　　　2 cups flour
Sprinkle of water if needed

Fresh Pasta[103]

Instructions

1. Make the basic pasta dough. Sift the flour onto a clean work surface and make a well in the center with your fist.
2. Break the eggs into the well and the water and a bit of salt.
3. Gradually mix the egg mixture into the flour using a fork, bringing the ingredients together into a firm dough. If the dough feels too dry, add a few drops of water; if it's too wet, add a little more flour. (You will soon grow accustomed to how the dough should feel after you've made it a few times.)
4. Knead the pasta until smooth, 2 to 5 minutes. Lightly massage it with a hint of olive oil, pop the dough into a plastic food bag, and allow it to rest at room temperature for at least 30 minutes. The pasta will be much more elastic after resting.
5. I actually now use a food processor to mix everything, then turn onto the counter to knead it until it feels firm enough to put through the machine.

---

[103] http://www.foodnetwork.com/recipes/ree-drummond/pantry-pasta-recipe-

Banana Breads   Kelly Beaton

Ingredients

3 ripe bananas
1 1/2 c flour
1 tsp baking soda
1 cup sugar

1 egg
1/4 cup butter - melted
1/4 tsp salt

Banana Breads

Instructions

1. Preheat over 350
2. Grease bread pan (9 inches)
3. Mash bananas until pureed.
4. Add butter, sugar, and egg and mix with electric beater.
5. In a separate bowl, mix 1 1/2 c flour, baking soda and salt.
6. Fold dry mixture into banana pureed mixture until completely blended.
7. Pour mixture into greased bread pan.
8. Bake for 50-60 minutes depending on the oven.
9. Option - can add nuts or chocolate chips or raisins

Bachelor Buttons — Mike Charrier

Ingredients

1 egg
1 cup brown sugar
1 tsp baking soda
1 cup filberts

1 cup butter
2 cups floor
½ tsp salt
1 cup cocoanut

Bachelor Buttons

Instructions

1. Mix as for cookies.
2. Form into small balls and place one half filbert or cherry in centre of each.
3. Bake at 300 to 335 ºF

Summer Pasta
Pamela DiNardo

Ingredients

2 tomatoes (chopped)
2 – 3 green onions, chopped
¼ cup fresh basil
1 tbsp mint (I use a ½ cup)
½ tsp salt
¼ tsp pepper
3 tbsp Olive Oil
½ cup mozzarella cheese

Summer Pasta[104]

Instructions

1. Cooked Pasta of choice, penne works the best.
2. Put all ingredients (except cheese) in small saucepan and heat, stir for 5 minutes.
3. Add cheese to hot pasta, stir to melt and mix.
4. Add the sauce.

---

[104] http://allrecipes.com/recipe/23445/rainbow-pasta-salad-

Ginger cookies (with crystallized ginger)   Corry Wink

Ingredients

1 cup butter at room temperature
1 egg
¼ tsp ground ginger
¾ tsp baking powder
½ cup finely chopped crystallized ginger

1 cup brown sugar
1 tsp vanilla
1½ cups all-purpose flour
½ tsp salt

Ginger cookies[105]

Instructions

1. In bowl, cream together butter and brown sugar. Beat in egg yolk, vanilla and gingers. Combine flour, baking powder and salt. Stir into butter mixture.
2. Drop batter by teaspoonful onto ungreased baking sheet. Bake at 350F for 10-12 minutes until just golden.
3. Cool on baking sheets for 5 minutes and then transfer to metal racks and cool completely. Makes 3 dozen cookies.

---

[105] https://www.bing.com/search?q=Triple+the+Ginger+Cookies

Cheesecake Cupcakes   Elinor Russell

Ingredients

24 paper muffin cups   1 cup sugar
2 tsp lemon juice   4 eggs
1 pkg vanilla wafers (I have used other flat round cookies as well)
3 9 oz pkgs cream cheese softened
Cherry, blueberry, or raspberry pie filling

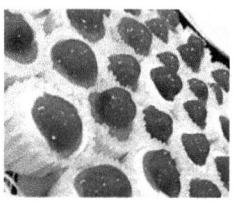

Cheesecake Cupcakes[106]

Instructions

1. Preheat oven to 350 degrees.
2. Mix sugar, cheese, eggs, and lemon juice until smooth.
3. Line muffin pans with papers.
4. Place one wafer in the bottom of each muffin cup. Spoon cheese mixture over wafers to fill cups 3/4 full.
5. Bake in preheated oven for 18 to 20 minutes.
6. Cool. Cupcakes will sink in the middle while cooling. Spoon pie filling on each cupcake and refrigerate at least one hour.
7. These may be topped with a whipped topping if desired. Serves 24.

---

[106] https://www.bing.com/search?q=Mini+Cheesecake+Cupcakes&filters

Recipes of Canadian Martyrs and St. Margaret Mary Church

Never Fail Flakey Pie Crust. Christine Andress
(From my grandmother, Theresa McNally)

Ingredients

5 cups flour
3/4 tsp salt
1 lb shortening
3 tbsp vinegar

3 tbsp brown sugar
1/2 tsp baking powder
1 egg
water

Never Fail Flakey Pie Crust[107]

Instructions

1. Sift flour and sugar, or at least break up the brown sugar in the flour to avoid clumps. Add salt and baking powder. Chop shortening into the flour until you have a fine meal mixture.
2. Break an egg into a measuring cup and add water until they have a combined volume of 3/4 cup. Add vinegar and stir. Add this to the flour and shortening mixture and stir with a fork. Roll onto a well floured board.
3. Chilling of the dough before rolling out is optional.
4. If using a food processor (which I do not, but my mother does), make half of the shortening and flour mixture, dump and then make the other half. Then add water and vinegar as usual.
5. Makes approximately 5 pie shells.

This family recipe has been making fantastic pies for three generations

---

[107]https://www.bing.com/search?q=Pie+Crust+Recipe&filters

No-longer Vegan Fettuccine   Christine Andress

Ingredients

1 tablespoon olive oil   1 tablespoon sugar
2 tablespoons balsamic vinegar   1 cup vegetable or chicken broth
Salt and pepper to taste
1 medium onion, sliced into half-moons
2 chicken breasts, cut into small pieces
1 cup sliced roasted red peppers (from a water-packed jar)
Fettuccine noodles
goat cheese as topping (optional, but really worth it!)

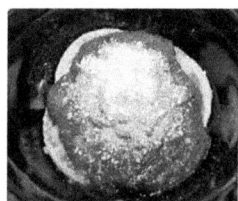

No-longer Vegan Fettuccine[108]

Instructions

1. Heat oil in a frying pan over medium heat. Add onions and sugar and cook, stirring a couple of times until onions are golden brown and caramelized. (Approx. 10-15 minutes).
2. In another large skillet, add more olive oil and cook the chicken over medium- high heat until no longer pink.
3. Add the roasted red peppers and onions to the chicken, stir in the balsamic vinegar and cook for 2 minutes. Add broth and simmer for a few more minutes.
4. Pour over fettuccine and top with goat cheese

The original recipe was vegan, but the lovely flavour seems to scream out for chicken and goat-cheese.

---

[108]https://www.bing.com/search?q=Easy+Homemade+Ravioli+Gluten+Free+Veg

Lemon Zucchini Bread
Nicole Lance

From *Two Peas in a Pod*

Ingredients

For the bread:
- 3 cups all-purpose flour
- 1 teaspoon baking soda
- 2 cups granulated sugar
- 3 large eggs
- 1 tablespoon fresh lemon juice
- 1 1/2 teaspoons vanilla extract
- 1 teaspoon salt
- 1 teaspoon baking powder
- Zest of 2 large lemons
- 1 cup light olive oil not extra-virgin
- 2 cups grated zucchini

For the lemon glaze:
- 2 cups powdered sugar
- 3 tablespoons fresh lemon juice

Lemon Zucchini Bread[109]

Instructions

1. Preheat oven to 325 degrees F. Grease and flour two 8 x 4-inch loaf pans. Set aside.
2. In a large bowl, whisk together the flour, salt, baking powder, and baking soda. Set aside.
3. In a medium bowl, combine sugar and lemon zest. Rub together with your fingers until fragrant.
4. In a large bowl, whisk together the lemon sugar mixture, eggs, olive oil, lemon juice, and vanilla. Whisk until smooth. Stir in the dry ingredients until combined, the batter will be thick. Stir in the zucchini and pour the batter into the prepared loaf pans.
5. Bake for 60-65 minutes, or until tester inserted in the center comes out clean.

---

[109]https://www.bing.com/search?q=Lemon+Zucchini+Bread&filters=ufn%3a%22Lemon+Zucchini+Bread

Recipes of Canadian Martyrs and St. Margaret Mary Church

6. Place the loaves on a cooling rack and cool for 15 minutes. Loosen the sides of the bread with a knife. Carefully remove the loaves from the pans. Let cool completely on rack.
7. While the bread is cooling, make the lemon glaze. In a small bowl, combine powdered sugar and lemon juice. Whisk until smooth. Drizzle the glaze over the loaves. Slice and serve.

Recipe Notes: This recipe makes TWO loaves. Can add blueberries. This moist lemon zucchini quick bread is topped with a sweet lemon glaze and is a summer favorite. Enjoy a slice for breakfast, as a snack, or dessert.
Prem time - 15 minutes
Total time - 1 hour 20 minutes
Cusine - American
Serving - 24

Pumpkin bread Angela Davis

Ingredients

Combine dry ingredients:
3 ½ cup flour
2 tsp baking powder
1 tsp nutmeg
½ tsp salt

2 tsp baking powder
1 tsp cinnamon
¼ tsp ground cloves

Pumpkin bread[110]

Instructions

1. Mix 1cup smooth pumpkin,
2. 1 cup oil,
3. 2/3 cup water
4. 4 eggs.
5. Add to 3 cups sugar.
6. Then ½ c chopped walnuts, with dry ingredients, 3 to 4 loaf pans. Bake 350°F for 1 hour.

---

[110] https://www.bing.com/search?q=Pumpkin+Bread&filter

Recipes of Canadian Martyrs and St. Margaret Mary Church

Vegetarian Casserole — Gina Downing

Ingredients

1 stalk celery, chopped	2 tbsp. oil
1 medium onion, chopped	1/4 tsp. salt
1 small green pepper, chopped	1/8 tsp. pepper
2 cups noodles	2 tbsp. cheddar cheese
6 oz. Monterey Jack cheese	1 cup broccoli
1/4 - ½ cup dry bread crumbs	½ cup milk
1 tbsp. wheat germ	1 tbsp. butter, melted

Vegetarian Casserole[111]

Instructions

1. Cook celery, onion, broccoli & green pepper in hot oil until tender but not brown.
2. Stir in noodles (cooked and drained), Monterey Jack cheese (shredded), milk, salt & pepper. Turn into an ungreased 1 ½ quart casserole. Bake, uncovered at 350 F for 15 minutes.
3. Top with combined crumbs, cheddar cheese, wheat germ & butter. Bake, uncovered for another 15 minutes.
   4 servings

---

[111] https://www.bing.com/search?q=Vegetarian+Mexican+Casserole&filters=uf n%3a%22Vegetarian+Mexican+Casserole%

Rice Casserole — Isobel Gordon

Ingredients

⅓ cup butter or margarine
1 tin onion soup
1 tin drained shrimp or drained mushrooms
1 tin consommé soup
1 cup. long grain rice

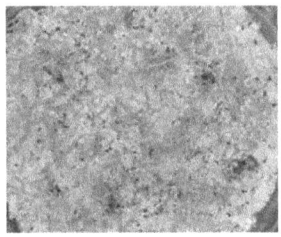

Rice Casserole[112]

Instructions

1. Mix and bake at 350 F for 1 hour (covered).
2. Stir occasionally. Serve hot.

---

[112]https://www.bing.com/search?q=Rice+Casserole&filters=ufn%3a%22Rice+Casserole

Gujerati Style Green Beans   Elizabeth Thorn

Ingredients

1 lb green beans
4 tbsp. corn oil
1 tbsp. black mustard seeds
½ tsp sugar

4 cloves garlic finely chopped
1 hot dried red chilli, crushed
1 tsp salt
½ tsp black pepper

Gujerati Style Green Beans[113]

Instructions

1. Blanch beans for 3-4 minutes or until they are tender. Then drain immediately in a colander and rinse under cold running water. Set aside.
2. Heat oil in a large frying pan over a medium heat. When hot put in the mustard seeds. As soon as the mustard seeds begin to pop, put in the garlic. Stir the garlic pieces until light brown.
3. Put in the red chili and stir for a few seconds. Put in the green beans salt and sugar. Stir to mix. Turn the heat to medium-low. Stir and cook the beans for 7-8 minutes or until they have absorbed the flavor of the spices.
4. Add pepper, mix and serve.

---

[113] https://www.bing.com/search?q=Smoked+Dal+Makhani+Recipe+-+Dhaba

Scallop Potatoes with Rosemary — Gen Gales

Ingredients

- 2 lbs potatoes
- 2 tbsp fresh or 1 tbsp dried rosemary
- 1 cup beef bouillon
- ½ clove garlic, crushed
- 1 cup grated Parmesan cheese
- tbsp butter

Scallop Potatoes with Rosemary[114]

Instructions

1. Preheat oven to 425 F. Rub a baking dish (about 10"x 2") with garlic and smear with 1 tbsp butter.
2. Spread a layer of potatoes, scrubbed, unpeeled and sliced. On the bottom of the dish, dot with butter, and sprinkle with some of the cheese. Repeat layers until potatoes are used up.
3. Sprinkle rosemary and remaining cheese over top. Pour on bouillon.
4. Bake 30 minutes or until potatoes are tender, bouillon has been absorbed and the top is golden brown.

---

[114] https://www.bing.com/search?q=LemonRosemary+Scalloped+Potatoes&filters

Vegetable Lasagna — Danielle De Banne

Ingredients

- 2 onions, chopped
- 2 cloves garlic, minced
- 1 sweet green pepper, chopped
- 14 oz can tomato sauce
- ¼ cup parsley
- 1tsp each oregano
- pinch crushed dried chilies
- 2 eggs
- pinch freshly grated nutmeg
- 1 lb mozzarella cheese, grated
- 2 tbsp olive oil
- ½ lb mushrooms, sliced
- 28 oz can plum tomatoes
- 2 carrots, shredded
- 1 tsp each dried thyme
- salt and pepper to taste
- 10 oz spinach
- 1 lb low fat ricotta cheese
- 1 cup grated Parmesan cheese

Vegetable Lasagna[115]

Instructions

1. Cook onions, garlic, green pepper and mushrooms in the oil for about 5 minutes. Add tomatoes and their juice, breaking up the tomatoes into small pieces. Add tomato sauce, carrots, parsley, herbs and spices.
2. Bring to a boil and simmer 30 minutes, stirring occasionally. Cook, drain and chop the spinach. In a food processor, whirl eggs, ricotta cheese, nutmeg and spinach until fairly smooth.
3. Spread 1/4 of the tomato sauce in the bottom of a greased 13"x9" baking dish. Then arrange a single layer of noodles, followed by 1/2 of the ricotta mixture, 1/4 of the tomato sauce, 1/3 of the mozzarella and 1/3 of the Parmesan. Repeat.
4. Arrange a final layer of noodles, the remaining tomato sauce and sprinkle with the remaining cheese. Bake at 350 F for 30 minutes, then covered for 15 minutes or until hot and bubbly. Let stand 10 minutes before serving. 10 servings

---

[115] https://www.bing.com/search?q=Easy+Vegetable+Lasagna&filters=ufn%3a%22Easy+Vegetable+Lasagna

Hash Brown Potato Casserole — Molly Fraser

Ingredient

2 lb. frozen hash browns
1 tsp pepper
1 can cream of chicken soup
2 cups grated cheddar cheese
2 cups cornflakes, crushed

1 tsp. salt
2-3 tbsp onion, chopped
1 ½ cups sour cream
½ cup butter, melted

Hash Brown Potato Casserole[116]

Instructions

1. In a large bowl, mix the ingredients of hash brown, salt, pepper, onions, chicken soup, sour cream and cheese. Place in a greased 9" x 13" pan. Sprinkle crushed cornflakes evenly over top of potato mixture. Drizzle with melted butter.
2. Cook 45 to 60 minutes in 350 F oven, or until lightly browned on top. May be prepared 1 or 2 days ahead and kept covered with foil for reheating.
3. Take foil off for last 10 minutes in the oven to make sure topping is crisp and brown.

---

[116] https://www.bing.com/search?q=Hash+Brown+Potato+Casserole&filters=ufn%3a%22Hash+Brown+Potato+Casserole

Recipes of Canadian Martyrs and St. Margaret Mary Church
African Winter Vegetable Stew　　　　　　　　Janet Bax

Ingredients

3 large sweet potatoes　　　　3 tbs. of vegetable or peanut oil
2 cups of onions　　　　　　　3 or 4 garlic cloves
2 cups chopped mushrooms　　2 cups diced carrots
2 cups cubed turnips　　　　　2 cups sliced parsnips
2 cups cubed eggplant　　　　2 cups cubed zucchini or squash
2 green peppers, chopped　　 2 chopped tomatoes
1 small can of tomato paste　 ½ tsp cayenne
½ tsp coriander　　　　　　　3 tbsp grated ginger root
½ cup vegetable stock　　　　1 cube vegetable bouillon
¼ cup miso　　　　　　　　　½ cup peanut butter
2 tbsp cider vinegar　　　　　2 cups tomato juice

African Winter Vegetable Stew[117]

Instructions
1. Boil the sweet potato cubes until they are tender (use the water to make your stock, if necessary). Sauté garlic, onions, ginger and spices in the oil for a couple of minutes.
2. Add mushrooms and continue to sauté for a couple more minutes. Add stock and bring to a boil, then add all vegetables except the sweet potatoes and cover and simmer for about 10-15 minutes. Make a paste of the peanut butter, miso (optional), vinegar and some of the tomato juice.
3. Add to the stew. Add sweet potatoes along with rest of tomato juice and simmer on low for about 10 more minutes. Do not let this stick.
4. Serve on rice or couscous.

---

[117] https://www.bing.com/search?q=African+Stew&filters=ufn%3a%22African+Stew

Zucchini-Cheese Casserole   Janet Bax

Ingredients

¾ cup bulgur or rice
2 cups onions
6 cups sliced zucchini
½ tsp basil
½ tsp black pepper
2 or 3 eggs
1 cup cottage cheese
2 tbsp of tomato paste
1 cup grated cheddar cheese
sesame seeds (optional)

2 ½ tsp oil
4 garlic cloves (peeled and diced)
½ tsp oregano
½ tsp marjoram
½ tsp curry powder
I cup of grated feta (5 ounces)
1 cup of parsley
1 tbsp of tamari or soy sauce
2 medium tomatoes, sliced

Zucchini-Cheese Casserole[118]

Instructions

1. Prepare bulgur or rice according to directions. .Sauté onions and garlic in oil for a couple of minutes. Add zucchini, herbs and pepper and sauté on medium heat until zucchini is tender but not soft. In a bowl, lightly beat eggs, and then mix in the feta and cottage cheese. Separately, mix chopped parsley, tomato paste, soy and the bulgur or rice. Two ways to assemble. Either put everything together in a casserole dish, if you are in a hurry, **or** layer, beginning with bulgur or rice mixture, then adding the sauté veggies, and then the feta and cottage cheese mixture. Top the casserole with grated cheddar, tomato slices and a sprinkle of sesame seeds.

---

[118]https://www.bing.com/search?q=Zucchini+%26+Cheese+Casserole&filters= ufn%3a%22Zucchini++Cheese+Casserole

Recipes of Canadian Martyrs and St. Margaret Mary Church

2   Bake either assembled casserole, covered, at 350 F for 45 minutes. If you like crunchy, crusty tops, uncover casserole for final 10-15 minutes. Served with a tossed green salad, this is really delicious, and very economical!!!

Penne with Artichokes and Feta — Frank Cedar

Ingredients

10 oz. dried Penne rigate
8 slices bacon
1 small onion, thinly sliced
9 oz artichoke
4 oz. (3/4 cup) feta cheese
3 tbsp chopped parsley

1 tbsp coarse salt
1 cup low-salt chicken broth
1/3 cup pitted olives, chopped
1 roasted red bell pepper,
1 tsp ground black pepper

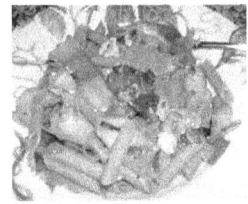

Penne with Artichokes and Feta[119]

Instructions

1. Bring a large pot of water to a full boil and add the pasta and 1 tbsp coarse salt. Cook until just tender, about 10 min. Drain and reserve. While the pasta is cooking, heat a large skillet (not non-stick) over medium-low heat.
2. Add the bacon and cook, turning occasionally, until brown and crisp, about 5 min. With tongs, transfer the bacon to a plate lined with paper towels. When cool, crumble into small pieces.
3. Add the sliced onion to the bacon drippings in the pan and cook over medium heat, stirring often, until wilted, about 3 min.
4. Add the quartered artichokes and cook, stirring occasionally, until the vegetables are tender and lightly browned on the edges, about another 4 min. Pour in the broth. Increase the heat to high and bring to a boil, scraping up all the browned bits in the pan. Boil for 30 seconds to reduce the liquid slightly. Reduce the heat to medium and add the drained pasta, olives, and red pepper.

---

[119] https://www.bing.com/search?q=Penne+with+Artichokes+%26+Feta&filters=ufn%3a%22Penne+with+Artichokes++Feta

5. Toss until well blended and warmed. Remove the pan from the heat. Add the crumbled feta and salt and pepper to taste and give the pasta a few stirs.
6. Cover and set aside, stirring occasionally, until the cheese melts a bit (but not completely) and the pasta is coated in creamy, clingy sauce, about 2 min. Taste and adjust the seasonings.
7. Serve immediately with the crumbled bacon and chopped parsley.

Potato and Carrot Casserole — Barbara Bareham

Ingredients

6 potatoes, grated
1 onion, grated
¼ cup rolled oats
3 tbsp vegetable oil
1 tsp salt
1 cup grated cheese

3 carrots, grated
1 cup skim milk powder
2 eggs
1 tsp garlic powder
1 tsp pepper

Potato and Carrot Casserole[120]

Instructions

1. Mix grated potatoes, carrots and onion in a large bowl.
2. Stir in skim milk powder, oats, eggs, oil, garlic powder, salt and pepper. Preheat oven to 350 F. Lightly grease 13" x 9" x 2" baking dish. Spread mixture evenly into the pan.
3. Bake for 30 to 40 minutes, or until potatoes are done. Sprinkle with cheese.
4. Return pan to oven for a few minutes to melt cheese.

---

[120] https://www.bing.com/search?q=Creamy+Potato+Carrot+Casserole&filters=ufn%3a%22Creamy+Potato+Carrot+Casserole

Recipes of Canadian Martyrs and St. Margaret Mary Church

Scalloped Potatoes — Barbara Bareham

Ingredients

- 1 tbsp margarine
- ¼ tsp garlic powder
- ½ tsp salt
- ¼ tsp oregano
- 2 tbsp seasoned bread crumbs
- 3 medium potatoes, thinly sliced
- ½ cup finely chopped onion
- 1 ½ cups milk
- ¼ tsp basil
- ¼ tsp ground pepper
- 2 tbsp grated cheese
- ¼ cup grated cheese

Seasoned Bread Crumbs:
- 1 cup fine, dry, bread crumbs
- 1 tbsp dried parsley
- ½ twp garlic powder
- 3 tbsp grated cheese
- 1 tsp dried oregano
- Salt and pepper

Mix all ingredients in a bowl and set aside for use in recipe below.

Scalloped Potatoes[121]

Instructions

1. Melt margarine in a small frying pan, over medium heat. Add onion and garlic powder. Cook until onion is soft (3-5 minutes) and set aside.
2. In a medium sized sauce pan, over medium heat, combine milk, salt, basil, oregano and pepper and warm (do not burn).
3. Combine seasoned bread crumbs and 2 tbsp cheese in a small bowl, then set aside. Preheat oven to 350 F.
4. Lightly grease an 8" x 8" x 2" casserole dish. Arrange 1/3 of the potatoes on the bottom of the dish.

---

[121] https://www.bing.com/search?q=Scalloped+Potatoes&filters=ufn%3a%22Scalloped+Potatoes

Recipes of Canadian Martyrs and St. Margaret Mary Church

5. Put half of the onion mixture on top of potatoes and sprinkle with half of the bread crumb mixture.
6. Next, put in half the remaining potatoes. Spread the rest of the onions and bread crumbs over the second potato layer.
7. Put the last third of the potatoes on top. Pour hot milk mixture into casserole. Sprinkle with remaining cheese. Cover and bake until potatoes are tender, about 50 to 60 minutes. 4 serving

Recipes of Canadian Martyrs and St. Margaret Mary Church

Spinach and Cheese Casserole   Barbara Bareham

Ingredients

1 package (10 oz.) fresh spinach
8 slices bread
1 cup grated cheese
1 ½ cups milk
½ tsp ground pepper

2 tbsp margarine
¼ cup finely chopped onion
3 eggs
1 tsp salt

Spinach and Cheese Casserole[122]

Instructions

1. Cut the coarse stems off the spinach and put the spinach leaves into a medium sized sauce pan, over medium heat. Add about ¼ cup hot water. Cover and cook for 2-3 minutes.
2. Rinse spinach with cold water and drain well. Lightly grease 8" x 8" x 2" baking dish. Spread margarine lightly on both sides of bread slices and place 4 slices on the bottom of the baking dish. Chop drained spinach and put into a medium bowl.
3. Add onion and cheese. Mix together. Spread mixture evenly over the bread.
4. Cut remaining 4 slices of bread into triangles, arrange over spinach mixture.
5. Combine eggs, milk, salt, pepper in medium bowl. Pour egg mixture over bread. Let stand 10 minutes. Bake for 50 to 60 minutes

---

[122]https://www.bing.com/search?q=Spinach+%26+Cheese+Casserole&filters=ufn%3a%22Spinach++Cheese+Casserole

Vegetable Side Dish — Barbara Bareham

Ingredients

1 large bunch broccoli
¾ cup finely chopped onion
1 cup milk
1 tsp salt
1 can (10 oz.) sliced mushrooms

2 tbsp margarine
2 tbsp flour
1 tsp Worcestershire sauce
1 tsp pepper
2 tbsp bread crumbs

Seasoned Bread Crumbs:
1 cup fine, dry, bread crumbs
1 tbsp dried parsley
½ tsp garlic powder
1 tsp pepper

3 tbsp grated cheese
1 tsp dried oregano
1 tsp salt

Mix all ingredients in a bowl and set aside for use in recipe below.

Vegetable Side Dish[123]

Instructions

1. Boil chopped broccoli, over high heat until crisp and tender (about 3-5 minutes). Drain and set aside. Melt margarine in a medium sized sauce pan, over medium heat. Add onion and cook until soft (about 3-5 minutes).
2. Stir in flour. Pour milk in slowly, stirring all the time. Cook and stir until mixture boils and thickens.
3. Add Worcestershire sauce.
4. Add salt and pepper to taste. Stir in broccoli and mushrooms. Preheat oven to 350 F. Put broccoli mixture into an 8" x 8" x 2" baking dish.

---

[123] https://www.bing.com/search?q=Southwest+Side+Dish&filters=ufn%3a%22Southwest+Side+Dish

Bake for 15 to 20 minutes, or until thoroughly heated. Sprinkle with seasoned bread crumbs and bake 5 minutes longer. 4 servings.

Salads

Jennifer Hegyi

Recipes of Canadian Martyrs and St. Margaret Mary Church

Hungarian Cucumber salad   Frank Hegyi

Ingredients

2 large cucumbers   3 tsp salt
1 bunch green onions   2 tsp paprika
3 tbsp oil   3 tbsp vinegar

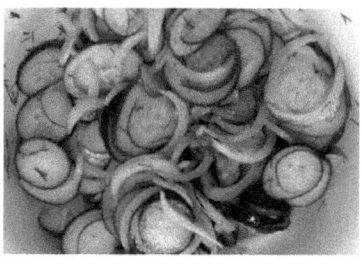

Hungarian Cucumber Salad

Instructions

1. Peel cucumbers and cut into thin slices (across). Put in a bowl and small pieces. Place onions in a small bowl, pour in oil and vinegar and season with paprika. Mix and let it stand for 15 minutes.
2. Remove cucumbers from bowl and squeeze the water out by hand. Empty water from the bowl and place the squeezed cucumber back.
3. Pour the onion mixture over the cucumbers and mix. Taste if it needs more oil or vinegar.

Pomegranite and Feta Salad — Kelly Langill

Ingredients

1 head romaine, washed and torn
1/2 cup crumbled feta cheese
1 bunch of baby spinach
1/4 cup toasted pinenuts
seeds of 1 pomegranite (or a small packet of craisens)

Dressing

1/3 cup olive oil
1 tbsp red wine vinegar
1 tsp dijon mustard
2 tbsp maple syrup
1/2 tsp oregano
salt and freshly ground peppers

Pomegranite and Feta Salad[124]

Instruction

1. Toss lettuce and spinach together in a large salad bowl.
2. Add the rest of the salad ingredients.
3. Whisk all dressing ingredients together and toss with salad just before serving.

---

[124]http://allrecipes.com/recipe/165076/pomegranate-feta-salad-with-lemon-dijon-

Recipes of Canadian Martyrs and St. Margaret Mary Church

BLT Chopped Salad with Corn, Feta and Avocado

Pamela DiNardo

Ingredients

2 cups butter lettuce, chopped
2 cups fresh arugula, chopped
1 pint grape tomatoes, halved
4 slices thick cut bacon, fried and crumbled
1 cup sweet corn
1 lime, juiced
4 oz feta, crumbled
1 avocado, chopped
1 ½ tbsp olive oil
¼ tsp salt
¼ tsp pepper

BLT Chopped Salad with Corn, Feta and Avocado[125]

Instructions

1. As a note, to chop my lettuce I like to lay it out on a big cutting board and just continuously run my knife through it (in all directions) until it is chopped as much as I like.
2. In a large bowl, combine lettuce, arugula, tomatoes, corn and avocado. Add in salt, pepper, olive oil and lime juice; then toss well to coat.
3. Fold in bacon and feta then divide evenly. If making ahead of time, cut and add the avocado just before serving.

---

[125] https://www.howsweeteats.com/2013/05/blt-chopped-salad-with-corn-feta-avocado

Mango Salad   Pamela DiNardo

Ingredients

1 or 2 mangos cut into ½ inch – 1 inch pieces
1 can black beans – rinsed and drained
¼ cup red onion – finely chopped
½ cup of cilantro – chopped
2 tbsp lime juice

1 avocado – chopped
1 can corn – drained
2 tbsp olive oil
¼ pineapple juice

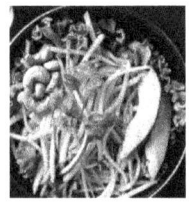

Mango Salad[126]

Instructions

1. Mix all ingredients together, adding the avocado last minute.
2. Mix last three ingredients together, pour over salad and toss.

---

[126] http://www.thekitchn.com/cool-recipe-thai-green-mango-s-123700

No Bake Key Lime Pie in a Jar — Pamela DiNardo

Ingredients

1 package graham crackers
1 (8 oz) package of cream cheese (softened)
Limes to garnish
2 tbsp butter (melted)
½ can condensed milk (7 oz)
½ cup plain or Greek Yogurt
4 small glass jars

No Bake Key Lime Pie in a Jar[127]

Instructions

1. The first thing you want to do is to crush up your graham crackers and mix them with 2 tbsp of butter. There are tons of ways to do this but I like putting them in my mini food processor and then adding the melted butter. Once you have done that, set it aside.
2. For the pie filling, combine your cream cheese, condensed mild, Greek yogurt and key lime juice in a stand mixer and mix on medium speed for about 5 minutes. If you don't have a stand mixer, whip vigorously with a whisk until you have a smooth, creamy texture. If you find your filling isn't as green as you would like add a drop or two of green gel coloring. Once mixed up, pop it into the fridge for about 10 minutes while you get the jars ready.
3. Now pour about 1/3 cup of the crushed graham crackers into the bottom of your jar and lightly pack them down. You don't want it to be too hard, so make sure it is just enough to stay in place.
4. After that take your filling mixture out of the fridge and pour about 2/3 cup into your jar and sprinkle on some more graham crackers. Now top it with some whipped topping and a slice of lime for garnish.

---

[127] http://millionmoments.net/2014/07/bake-key-lime-pie-jar.htm

Broccoli Salad
Pamela DiNardo

Ingredients

1 broccoli (chopped)
1 cup raisins soaked in water
¾ cup sunflower seeds (unsalted)
¾ cup grated onion

1 cup mayonnaise
1 tsp sugar
1 tsp vinegar

Broccoli Salad[128]

Instructions

1. Mix all ingredients together.
2. This salad is best made and then let to rest for 4-12 hours.
3. Even better if you can make it the day before and keep in the fridge wrapped.

---

[128] http://allrecipes.com/recipe/14280/fresh-broccoli-salad/

Grilled Zucchini & Buffalo Mozzarella Salad
Pamela DiNardo

Ingredients

4 small zucchinis, each about 6 inches long
1 tbsp lemon juice
½ tsp dried chilli flakes
15 oz ball buffalo mozzarella
grilling
Salt and freshly ground pepper
1 tsp lemon zest
¼ cup extra virgin olive oil, plus extra for
Handful of fresh basil leaves

Grilled Zucchini & Buffalo Mozzarella Salad[129]

Instructions

1. Trim the stem end of the zucchini and slice each lengthwise into several thin slices. Toss the cut zucchini with just enough olive oil to lightly coat, and grill over high heat until softened and lightly charred. Remove to a shallow serving platter. (try not to overcook the zucchini, you don't want it mushy)
2. To make the dressing, combine the olive oil, chili flakes, lemon juice and zest and season to taste with salt and pepper.
3. Using your fingers, tear mozzarella into small bite-size pieces and scatter over the grilled zucchini.
4. Spoon dressing over the salad, lightly toss, and top with a handful of the fresh basil leaves.

---

[129]tts://images.search.yahoo.com/yhs/search?p=Grilled+Zucchini+%26+Buffalo+

"Salade d'amour" — Pauline Willey

Ingredients

1 cup instant brown rice cooked
¼ cup green onions, minced
¼ cup carrots, shredded
¼ cup cucumber, diced
Dressing:
1 tsp sesame oil
3 tbsp soy sauce
2 tbsp maple syrup

¼ cup cashew
¼ cup red peppers, diced
¼ cup bean sprouts
1 cup baby spinach

¼ cup Omega-3 oil
1 tbsp lemon juice

Salade d'amour[130]

Instructions

1. Mix the salad ingredients in a large bowl.
2. Put the dressing ingredients in a small bowl and whip with fork.
3. Dress the salad and enjoy!

---

[130] http://s3-ca-central-1.amazonaws.com/staging-praticopratiques/app/uploads/sites/

Mexican Salad Bowl   Cornelius Kroon

Ingredients

1 lb lean ground beef. Cook over medium heat for about 10 minutes breaking up large chunks of beef.
1 clove of garlic crushed   1 can tomatoes diced
1 tsp salt   ½ tsp pepper
½ tsp turmeric   ¼ package taco spices

Mexican Salad Bowl[131]

Instructions

1 Add all above ingredients to the meat and let simmer for 30 minutes or until most of the liquid has been absorbed (Before doing this step, I removed some of the liquid fat from fried beef)
2 Chop a head of Iceberg lettuce and place in glass bowl.
3 Place cooked meat on top of lettuce bed (make it look like a nest)
4 Chop: 1 bunch of green onion, using some of the green, many small tomatoes in half, 1 red pepper diced in small pieces, spread over cooked meat.
5 Top with 1 cup shredded cheddar spread and a few pieces of sliced green onions.
6 Serve with nacho corn chips and sour cream and salsa. Enjoy!

---

[131]https://www.bing.com/search?q=Mexican+Salad+Bowl&filters=ufn%3a%22Mexican+Salad+Bowl%

Spicy Chili — Janice Cameron-Caluori

Ingredients

- 1 lbs bacon, chopped
- 1 head garlic, separated, peeled, sliced
- 2 chopped red peppers
- 3-5 heaping spoonfuls chili powder
- 2 28oz cans whole tomatoes
- 1 19oz can kidney beans
- 2 whole onions, chopped
- 2 lbs ground beef
- 1 19oz can black beans
- 1 19oz can kidney beans
- Salt and pepper

Spicy Chili[132]

Instructions

1. Heat a large pot over medium-high heat and add bacon.
2. Add a splash of water and let the bacon render its fat. As the water evaporates, the bacon will brown. Pour off the excess fat and add the onions, garlic, and peppers.
3. Cook until they are softened and just beginning to caramelize.
4. Add chili powder and ground beef and stir well, chopping the beef up with a wooden spoon.
5. Add tomatoes and beans and season with salt and pepper.
6. Simmer for an hour.

If you have the time, make this a day ahead and reheat when needed. The flavours will brighten and meld as it rests overnight.

---

[132] https://www.bing.com/search?q=Spicy+Beef+Chili&filters=ufn%3a%22Spicy+Beef+Chili-

Garden-fresh Corn Salad — Janice Cameron-Caluori

Ingredients

3 cups raw corn kernels (about 4 cobs)   ¼ cup olive oil
1 medium tomato, chopped   ¾ cup green onion, chopped
1 cup cucumber, quartered and sliced
½ cup radishes, chopped   ½ cup fresh herbs, chopped
1 medium jalapeno, very thinly sliced (optional)
1 tbsp red wine vinegar or white wine vinegar
2 cloves garlic, minced   ½ tsp salt
Ground pepper, to taste   1 ripe avocado, diced
1/3 cup crumbled feta cheese

Garden-fresh Corn Salad[133]

Instructions

1. In a large serving bowl, combine the corn, tomato, green onion, cucumber, herbs, radishes, and jalapeno.
2. In a liquid measuring cup or small bowl, combine the olive oil, vinegar, garlic, salt, and pepper. Whisk until blended, then pour over the salad. Toss to combine.
3. Add most of the feta and avocado (reserve some for garnish) and gently toss. Taste, and add more vinegar for more tang or salt for more overall flavour. Garnish with remaining cheese and avocado.
4. Serve promptly or chill for later. This salad keeps well for 3 to 4 days in the refrigerator, covered.

---

[133] https://www.bing.com/search?q=Garden-Fresh+Corn+Salad

Holiday Salad — Elinor Russell

Ingredients

8 plum tomatoes-seeded, chopped
6 celery stalks- sliced diagonally
1 cup kalamata olives -pitted
3 peppers-red/orange/yellow- bite size pieces
2 -170 g marinated artichokes-coarsely chopped
½ cup fresh dill - coarsely chopped (I have used freeze dried dill)
1 small red onion
2 oranges

Dressing:
1 lemon
2 tsp Dijon mustard
2 tsp dried dill weed
½ tsp each of basil, salt, and pepper
2 tbsp sugar
2 cloves garlic, minced
1/3 cup olive oil

Holiday Salad[134]

Instructions

1. Peel oranges: cut in half, then slice into half-moon shaped pieces.
2. Combine tomatoes, celery, peppers, onion, artichokes, oranges, olives, and dill in large bowl.
3. Squeeze 1/4 cup lemon juice into a small bowl.
4. Whisk in sugar, Dijon mustard, garlic, dillweed, basil, salt, and pepper.
5. Drizzle dressing over vegetables and serve.

---

[134] https://www.bing.com/search?q=Make+Ahead+Holiday+Salad&filters

Recipes of Canadian Martyrs and St. Margaret Mary Church

Quinoa Salad with Peaches and Pickled Onion
Elinor Russell

Ingredients

1 ½ cup quinoa, rinsed well   4 tsp salt
1 medium red onion, thinly sliced   3 tbsp sugar
½ cup apple cider vinegar   1/4 cup olive oil
2 large ripe firm peached, cut into ½ inch pieces
½ bunch arugula, thick stems trimmed, leaves torn (about 2 cups freshly
Ground pepper   2 cups small cherry tomatoes, halved
½ cup ½ inch pieces chives, divided

Quinoa salad

Instructions

1. Bring quinoa and 4 cups water to a boil in a medium saucepan. Season with salt. Cover reduce heat and simmer until quinoa is tender, 8 to 10 minutes. Drain, return quinoa to pa n and cover. Remove from heat and let sit 15 minutes. Fluff with a fork and spread out on a rimmed baking sheet; let coll.
2. Meanwhile, place onion ion a small bowl. Bring vinegar, sugar and 4tsp salt to a boil in a pot, stirring to dissolve. sugar and salt. Drain. Reserving pickling liquid
3. Toss pickled onion, peaches, arugula, tomatoes, oil, 1/4 cup chives and 3 tbsp reserved pickling liquid in a large bowl. Season with salt and pepper and more pickling liquid if desired Serve Salad topped with remaining chives.

(Feel free to use cooked bulgur, barley, or couscous instead of quinoa)

Cold Chicken Salad — Jean Cunliffe

Ingredients

- 4 cups chicken breasts
- 2 cups celery, sliced
- 2 cups seedless grapes
- 1 tsp pepper
- 1 tsp curry (optional)
- 2 tbsp lemon juice
- 1 cup slivered salted almonds
- 1 tsp salt
- 1 cup mayonnaise

Cold Chicken Salad[135]

Instructions

1. Cook chicken the day before serving and add lemon juice. Refrigerate.
2. Next morning add celery, grapes cut in halves, and mayonnaise.
3. Season with salt and pepper and chill.
4. Before serving, add toasted almonds and toss well. Sprinkle with paprika or parsley.

---

[135] https://www.bing.com/search?q=Cold+Chicken+Pasta+Salad&filters=ufn%3a%22Cold+Chicken+Pasta+Salad

24 Hour Salad
Olive Laforce

Ingredients

½ pint whipped cream
3 tbsp. white vinegar
2 tbsp. butter
1 tin (14 oz.) pineapple tidbits
2 cup miniature marshmallows

2 eggs, beaten
4 tbsp. white sugar
1 or 2 tins mandarin oranges
1 cup grapes

24 Hour Salad[136]

Instructions

1. Drain all fruit well. Place eggs in a double boiler with sugar and vinegar. Beat and stir until thick and smooth.
2. Remove from heat and add butter.
3. Place in refrigerator and chill completely.
4. Fold in whipped whipping dream; add fruit, then marshmallows. (Better if chilled 24 hours before serving.)

---

[136] https://www.bing.com/search?q=Broccoli+Salad&filters=ufn%3a%22Broccoli+Salad

Orange Pecan Salad — Frank Cullen

Ingredients

1 head of romaine lettuce
2 oranges

1 cup of pecans

Orange Pecan Salad[137]

Instructions

1. Blend lettuce, pecans (toasted and chopped), and oranges (peeled and cut in small pieces).
2. Add dressing of vinegar, sugar, oil, salt, onions, mustard and water and add to salad.
3. Blend until well mixed. Refrigerate and serve.

---

[137] https://www.bing.com/search?q=Cranberry+Pecan+Salad&filters=ufn%3a%22Cranberry+Pecan+Salad

Curried Lentil salad
Louise Rickenbacker

Ingredients

½ cup wild rice
½ cup orzo
¼ cup chopped red onion
Dressing:
¼ cup white wine vinegar
1 tsp ground cumin
½ tsp granulated sugar
½ tsp ground coriandar
¼ tsp paprika
¼ tsp ground cardamon
pinch cloves
¼ cup vegetable oil

⅔ cup green or brown lentils
½ cup currants
⅓ cup slivered almonds, toasted

2 tbsp. water
1 tsp Dijon mustard
½ tsp salt
¼ tsp turmeric
¼ tsp ground nutmeg
pinch cinnamon
pinch cayenne pepper

Curried Lentil salad[138]

Instructions

1. In separate pots of boiling water, cook wild rice for 35 to 40 minutes, lentils for 25 to 30 minutes and orzo for 5 minutes or until each is tender but not mushy.
2. Drain well and transfer to a large bowl.
3. Add currants and onion; set aside. 4 servings.
4. Dressing: in small bowl, whisk together vinegar, water, cumin, mustard, sugar, salt, coriander, turmeric, paprika, nutmeg, cardamon, cinnamon, cloves and cayenne; whisk in oil. Pour over rice mixture and toss gently. Let cool completely. Cover and refrigerate for at least 4 hours. Serve sprinkled with almonds. May be refrigerated up to 2 days.

---

[138] https://www.bing.com/search?q=Curried+Lentil+Salad&filters=ufn%3a%

Orange Poppy Seed Salad — Louise Rickenbacker

Ingredients

Dressing:
½ clove garlic
1 tsp poppyseeds
1 tsp dry mustard
1 cup salad oil

⅓ cup vinegar (white or cider)
½ cup sugar
1 tsp salt

Orange Poppy Seed Salad[139]

Instructions

1. Drop garlic into food processor or blender; mince. Add remaining ingredients except oil and combine.
2. Add oil in a thin stream while blending; dressing will become quite thick.
3. Store dressing in a jar in the refrigerator until ready to use.

Salad:

1 head romaine lettuce, washed, dried and torn into bite-sized pieces
1 tin mandarin oranges, drained   1/2 cup slivered almonds.

1. Toss almonds in a small frying pan, under the broiler or in microwave until lightly browned.
2. Toss lettuce, oranges and almonds in a large salad bowl, adding just enough dressing to moisten (about half the dressing). Serve immediately.

---

[139] https://www.bing.com/search?q=Orange-Poppy+Seed+Salad&

Chinese Salad
Shona Timmins

Ingredients

2 cups cooked rice
½ lb bean
1 cup raw, sliced mushrooms
3 stalks of chopped celery
¼ cup soya sauce
1 clove minced garlic

½ packet of raw spinach
1 cup cashews
½ cup chopped green onions
3 sprigs parsley
½ cup vegetable oil

Chinese Salad[140]

Instructions

1. Mix ingredients: rice, spinach, beans, cashews, mushrooms, green onion, celery and parsley 1 hour prior to serving
2. Mix dressing: soya sauce, oil and garlic and toss over salad, and refrigerate.

---

[140]https://www.bing.com/search?q=Chinese+Salad&filters=ufn

Thai Pear Salad — Barbara Fischer

Ingredients

Salad:
2 Japanese pears
1 hot red pepper
Carrot bits
5 tbsp. chopped coriander
½" chunk of fresh ginger
Celery bits

Dressing:
¼ cup of rice vinegar
⅛ cup of lime juice

Thai Pear Salad[141]

Instructions

1. Chop Japanese pears into slivers.
2. Finely dice carrot and celery.
3. Chop pepper, coriander and ginger.
4. Mix the chopped ingredients in a small bowl.
5. Just before serving, add the dressing and mix well.

---

[141] https://www.bing.com/search?q=Spicy+Thai+Papaya+Salad&filters=ufn%3a%22Spicy+Thai+Papaya+Salad

Bean Salad   Jean Burke

Ingredients

1 can 4 oz green bean
1 can 14oz yellow waxed beans
1 can 14 oz red kidney beans
½ cup minced onion
¼ cup cider vinegar

1 can 14 oz lima beans
¼ cup salad oil
¼ tsp. pepper
½ cup green pepper
⅜ cup white sugar

Bean Salad[142]

Instructions

1 Mix oil, vinegar, pepper and sugar and pour over beans. Mix well to marinate beans.
2 Refrigerate overnight, Use a slotted spoon to serve.
3 Drain kidney beans but save liquid and add to marinade. 8 servings

---

[142] https://www.bing.com/search?q=Three+Bean+Salad&filters=ufn%3a%22Three+Bean+Salad

Cranberry Pear Relish   Barb Popel

Ingredients

4 cups fresh or frozen cranberries
2 cups water
1 jalapeno pepper
3 tbsp lime juice

1 ½ cups brown sugar,
2 cups Bosc or Asian pears
1 cup golden raisins

Cranberry Pear Relish[143]

Instructions

1. Heat the cranberries, sugar and water to boiling. Simmer, stirring occasionally, until the cranberries start to pop and release their juices.
2. Add the peeled and diced pears, seeded and minced jalapeno pepper, raisins and lime juice.
3. Simmer another 5 minutes. Remove from heat. Cool and serve at room temperature

---

[143] https://www.bing.com/search?q=Cranberry-Pear+Relish&filters=ufn%3a%22Cranberry-Pear+Relish

Herb-Glazed Brussels Sprouts   Barb Popel

Ingredients

¼ cup chopped fresh mint
¼ cup olive oil
1 tbsp Dijon mustard
¼ tbsp black pepper

¼ cup chopped fresh basil
3 tbsp lemon juice
¼ tbsp. salt
1 lbs. small Brussels sprouts

Herb-Glazed Brussels sprout

Instructions

1. Clean sprouts and make a slit on the bottom of each.
2. Whisk together all the other ingredients. Cook sprouts in boiling salted water for 3-5 minutes, until bright green.
3. Drain and spoon dressing over.

Green Bean and Walnut Salad — Kelly Adams

Ingredients

1 lb. green beans
4 tsp. Freshly grated parmesan cheese
1 onion, finely chopped
1 garlic clove, chopped

dressing:
6 tbsp. Olive oil
salt and pepper
2 tbsp. Chopped walnuts
2 tsp. White wine vinegar
2 tsp. chopped fresh tarragon

Green Bean and Walnut Salad

Instructions

1. Trim the beans but leave them whole. Cook for 3-4 minutes in lightly salted boiling water. Drain well and run under cold water. Drain again and pour into a mixing bowl. Add onion, garlic and cheese.
2. Place all dressing ingredients in a jar with a screw-top lid. Shake well and then pour the dressing over the salad. Toss gently to coat and cover with a plastic wrap and chill for at least half an hour.
3. Remove the beans from the fridge @ 10 minutes. before serving and give them a quick stir. Place in a serving dish. Toast the nuts in a dry skillet or under the broiler. Sprinkle the toasted nuts over the beans to garnish immediately before serving.

Recipes of Canadian Martyrs and St. Margaret Mary Church

Byward Maple Parsnips — Barb Popel

Ingredients

8 parsnips, peeled and cut into sixths
maple syrup
thyme

butter
a little water

Byward Maple Parsnips

Instructions

1. Preheat oven to 375 F.
2. Place parsnips in a baking dish, dot generously with butter, drizzle with maple syrup, and add a little water to the dish.
3. Cover with foil and bake for about 25 minutes, or until the parsnips are tender but not mushy.
4. Sprinkle with fresh thyme or tarragon (optional). 4 servings.

Blue Cheese Salad Dressng   Margaret Tansey

Ingredients

1 large clove garlic
1 tbsp blue cheese
1 tsp Dijon mustard
2 tbsp red wine vinegar
1 tsp salt
1 tbsp fresh lemon juice
1 tbsp mayonnaise
1 tbsp oil

Blue Cheese Salad Dressing

Instructions

1. Put garlic and salt into a food processor, whiz until combined.
2. Add remaining ingredients and process until smooth. Transfer to a jar and keep in the frig.
3. Makes enough for three family sized salads.
4. Alternate method: Crush garlic and salt together in medium bowl add cheese and mash into salt/garlic mixture.
5. Add remaining ingredients and combine. Store in a jar in the frig, shake well before using.

Thai Grilled Beef Salad   Chamchun Zisk

Ingredients

- 8 cups red and/or white cabbage
- 3 fish sauce (nam pla)*
- 2 large shallots, thinly sliced
- ½ cup chopped fresh cilantro
- 3 tbsp minced lemongrass*
- 5 tbsp fresh lime juice
- 2 small rib-eye steaks
- ½ cup green onion
- ½ cup sliced fresh mint
- 1 tsp minced Thai chile

Thai Grilled Beef Salad

Instructions

1. Grilled rib eyes are sliced and tossed with mint, lemongrass, chili, and lime juice, then served atop a marinated cabbage mixture in this main-course salad.
2. Combine thinly sliced cabbage, 2 tbsp lime juice and 1 tbsp fish sauce in large bowl; toss to blend.
3. Season with salt and pepper; set cabbage mixture aside for up to 30 minutes.
4. Prepare barbecue (medium-high heat). Sprinkle steaks with salt and pepper. Grill until cooked to desired doneness, 3 minutes per side for medium-rare.
5. Transfer steaks to work surface; cut crosswise into thin slices. Place sliced steaks in large bowl. Add shallots, onion tops, cilantro, mint, lemongrass, and chili, then remaining 3 tbsp lime juice and 2 tbsp fish sauce. Toss to blend. Season salad with salt and pepper.
6. Divide cabbage mixture among 4 plates. Top each with beef salad.

Dips and Spread

Kelly Langill

Pam Dixon

Satay Pork with Peanut Sauce   Kelly Langill

Ingredients

1 cup whipping cream or yogurt
1/2 small onion chopped
4 cloves garlic chopped
1 1/2 tsp salt

1 1/2 tsp ground cumin
4 tsp curry powder
1/2 tsp cayenne pepper

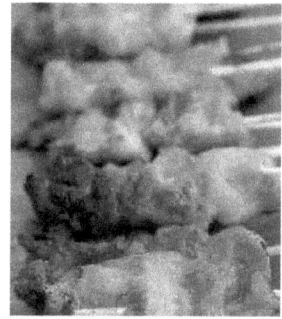

Marinade. Use this in the next recipe, chicken or pork.

Recipes of Canadian Martyrs and St. Margaret Mary Church

Chicken or pork, cut into cubes — Kellie Langill

Ingredients

Chicken or pork, cut into cubes
Salty pork sauce:
1/3 cup peanut butter
1/3 cup water
1 clove garlic
dash of cayenne pepper

2 tbsp lime juice
2 tbsp soya sauce
2 tsp sugar

Chicken or pork, cut into cubes[144]

Instructions

1. Mix marinade ingredients well.
2. Put meat in a large ziploc bag and add the marinade. Marinade at room temperature for 15 minutes.
3. Place meat evenly spread on a baking sheet and cook under the broiler.
4. Whip the sauce ingredients together.
5. Serve meat on top of a bed of rice. Spoon sauce over the meat.

---
[144] http://www.yummyhunts.com/recipes/Pork-and-Chicken-Afritada-2016

Recipes of Canadian Martyrs and St. Margaret Mary Church

Crabmeat Spread — Elinor Russell

Ingredients

2 tbsp Mayonnaise
garlic juice or powder
1 tbsp Worcestershire sauce
1 tbsp lemon juice
onion juice or grated onion
250 g cream cheese

Crabmeat Spread[145]

Instructions

1. Mix until smooth. Spread mixture on a large glass plate.
2. Spread chile sauce over the mixture.
3. Over this spread 1 can of crabmeat (shrimp may be used)

[145] https://www.bing.com/search?q=Crab+Spread&filters=ufn%3a%22Crab+

Fried Noodles — Angela Davis

Ingredients

2-3 bunches of Chinese noodles
Either buy fresh or cook in water for 8 minutes. Set aside to drain.
½ lb bacon, fry and set aside fat.

Fry in bacon fat:
2 c green onion
1 head bok choy
Barbecue sliced pork from Asian store.
1 lb mushrooms chopped or sliced

Crushed garlic
1 lb ground pork
Cooked bacon

Fried Noodles[146]

Instructions

1. Combine 2 tbsp corn starch and 1 c water.
2. Add 1 tbsp Mushroom soy.
3. Pour over fried meats and vegetables. Cook and stir until combined.

Fry cooked rice noodles.

4. Add 2 tsp fish gravy. Essential but add at last minute. It smells badly but not smelly when added at the end.

---

[146] https://www.bing.com/search?q=Fried+Noodles&filters=ufn%3a%22Fried+

Tabouli   Gina Downing

Ingredients

4 oz of parsley, washed drained and chopped
8 green onions - chopped and rubbed with a little salt
4 tomatoes - seeded and chopped
1 medium cucumber -seeded and chopped
⅔ cup lemon juice   ⅔ cup olive oil
salt and pepper to taste
½ cup of cracked wheat - washed, soaked for ½ hour, and drained.

Tabouli

Instructions

1   Mix all ingredients together. Let stand for ½ hour before serving.
2   Note: rubbing onions and salt together before mixing with other ingredients will allow the Tabouli to remain fresh for a couple of days. 4 servings.

Asparagus Dip
Gina Downing

Ingredients

- 1-8 oz. pkg. Cream cheese
- ¼ cup mayonnaise
- 2 tsp. curry powder
- 2 tbsp. Chopped parsley
- salt and pepper to taste
- ½ cup sour cream
- 15 oz. can green asparagus tips
- ½ pkg. dry French onion soup mix
- 1 tsp. prepared mustard

Asparagus Dip

Instructions

1. Beat cream cheese, sour cream and mayonnaise until smooth.
2. Drain asparagus and chop.
3. Add to cream cheese mixture.
4. Mix in rest of ingredients and season with salt and pepper. Refrigerate at least 4 hours before serving.

Pineapple Cream Fruit Dip — Elaine Borg

Ingredients

½ cup pineapple juice
¼ c. sugar
1 egg, slightly beaten

1 tbsp cornstarch
1 tbsp lemon juice
125 g. softened cream cheese

Pineapple Cream Fruit Dip

Instructions

1. Mix first pineapple juice, sugar, cornstarch and lemon juice in sauce pan.
2. Cook over medium heat, stirring constantly for about 5 minutes until clear and thickens. Slowly stir some hot mixture into egg.
3. Return this to pan and continue to cook over low heat until it slightly thickens. Cool about 5 minutes.
4. Whisk in cream cheese until smooth.
5. Refrigerate at least 2 hours prior to serving with fruit of your choice to dip into it.

Recipes of Canadian Martyrs and St. Margaret Mary Church

Herbed Vegetable Dip   Elaine Borg

Ingredients

3 cloves of garlic
black olives
1cup of fresh herbs, such as parsley, rosemary, thyme, basil, chives

anchovies to taste
black pepper
1 cup of olive oil.

Herbed Vegetable Dip

Instructions

1   In blender, combine the above listed ingredients.

Recipes of Canadian Martyrs and St. Margaret Mary Church

Salsa
Vania Gomez

Ingredients

2 cups chopped tomatoes
1 sweet yellow pepper, diced
2 cloves garlic, minced
¼ tsp. hot pepper sauce
tortilla chips

4 green onions chopped fine
2 tbsp. chopped coriander
2 tbsp. lime juice
salt and pepper
1 green pepper, sliced

Salsa

Instructions

1 In a bowl, combine tomatoes, peppers, onions, garlic, parsley, lime juice, hot pepper sauce and salt and pepper to taste.
2 Using slotted spoon, spoon over cheese dip cake.
3 Serve with tortilla chips. (Blue chips make a nice colour contrast) Chips can be placed on the platter around the cheese dip cake.

Hot Crab Dip   Sheila Gasnick

Ingredients

1 large package cream cheese	1 tbsp mayonnaise
1 tsp lemon juice	1 tsp horseradish
1 can crab meat	1 small onion
salt	pepper
½ tsp curry powder	1 package Swiss cheese

Hot Crab Dip

Instructions

1 Mix together above ingredients.
2 Place half the crab mixture on bottom, put a layer of cheese chunks, put another half of crab mixture, then put Swiss cheese chunks on top.
3 Bake at 350 F until it bubbles (approximately 15-20 minutes).
4 Serve hot with Swiss cheese crackers.

Desserts

Heather and Joseph Duggan

Patrick Zdunich

Hungarian Palacsinta   Frank Hegyi

Ingredients

5 cups of sifted flour
4 eggs separated (yolk/white)
2 cups milk
2 cups cottage cheese
2 tbsp sugar

1 tsp salt
2 cups carbonated water
¼ lb butter
1 egg yolk
½ cup sour cream

Hungarian Palacsinta

Instructions

1. Mix in a bowl flour, egg yolks, salt and 1 cup of milk, stirring until smooth. Gradually stir in the rest of the milk to make a batter with consistency of heavy cream.
2. Beat egg whites until stiff but not dry and fold into the batter. Stir again and let it stand for 30 minutes.
3. Heat an 8 inch frying pan. When the pan is hot, add ¼ tsp of butter and let it melt until covers the bottom of the pan.
4. Pour a ladle of the batter into the pan and gently move the pan around so that the batter covers the entire pan, almost paper thin. When the top of the batter bubbles, turn the pancake over and cook for 4 or 5 seconds longer.
5. Remove the cooked pancake and place flat on a plate. Continue until batter is all cooked, add butter into the pan for each pancake.
6. Mash cottage cheese until well creamed. Mix with egg yolk, sugar and cream. Place each pancake on a clean plate, put 1 tbsp cheese mixture in the centre, then roll it up.
7. Place all rolled up pancakes in a baking dish and heat in oven under 350 F for 20 minutes

English trifle   Sheila Gasnick

Ingredients

1 small raspberry jello
¼ cup sherry (optional)
1 pint Custard
2 tbsp. icing sugar

1 yellow loaf cake
½ cup raspberries
2 cans or Vanilla pudding
500 ml. whipping cream

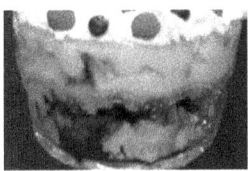

English Trifle[147]

Instructions

1. Start 1 day ahead. First day, prepare jello and set aside. Cut cake into 3 long slices. Spread with raspberry jam, reassemble, then cut into cubes. Place in glass serving bowl. Sprinkle cake with sherry. Spread raspberries over cake. Pour jello over cake. Cover and refrigerate.
2. Next Day, prepare custard according to directions and spread over cake mixture. Cover. Refrigerate until needed. Just before Serving, whip whipping cream until thick.
3. Add icing sugar to sweeten cream. Spread as much cream as desired over custard. Decorate as desired.

---

[147] http://allrecipes.com/recipe/8445/english-trifle/

Shortbread Cookies
Pamela DiNardo

Ingredients

½ cup corn starch   ½ cup icing sugar
1 cup sifted flour   1 cup butter

This are melt in your mouth made by my Auntie Millie.

Shortbread Cookies

Instructions

1. Sift corn starch and sugar into a bowl. Have butter at room temperature. Blend butter into dry ingredients with a spoon.
2. Shape into balls about an inch in diameter, about an inch apart. Press with fork onto un-greased baking sheet, press a piece of candied cherry, red or green for festive colours into the centre.
3. Bake slow oven 275-300 degrees for 8 – 10 minutes

Recipes of Canadian Martyrs and St. Margaret Mary Church

Lebanese knafeh jibneh with orange blossom syrup

Nicholas Hafez

Ingredients

For the orange blossom syrup
1 1/2 cups sugar
3/4 cups water
For the pastry
1/2 package shredded phyllo knafeh dough (kataifi),
1 cup panko or plain dry breadcrumbs
1/4 cup (2 sticks) unsalted butter,   2 cups whole milk melted
1/3 cup farina (cream of wheat)   1/2 cup orange blossom syrup
2 cups shredded mozzarella or ackawi cheese
1/4 cup pistachios, chopped, for serving

1 tbsp lemon juice
2 tsp orange blos

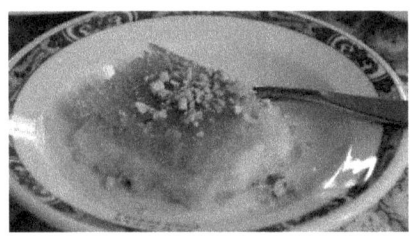

Lebanese knafeh jibneh

Instructions

1 To make the orange blossom syrup, in a small heavy saucepan, combine sugar, water and lemon juice and bring to a boil over medium high heat. Reduce heat to low and simmer for 5 minutes. Add the orange blossom water, pour into a heatproof container, cool to room temperature and refrigerate to chill.

2 In the food processor, pulse the shredded phyllo dough for about a minute to make it into a fine meal. Place the phyllo in a medium bowl with the breadcrumbs. Add the melted butter and ½ cup of orange blossom syrup and stir until the phyllo is completely coated.

3 In a 10-inch pie plate or cake pan (or a similar sized sheet pan), add the buttery dough mixture. Compress it very well by pushing it into the

4   bottom of the pan firmly, first with your hands, then pressing with the flat bottom of a cup, or something similar.

5   If the cheese is too salty, slice and soak it in cold water until some of the salt is pulled out. Change the water every 10 minutes or so. Either with a large, sharp knife or in the food processor, chop the cheese to a fine dice (in the processor, pulse until the cheese looks like coarse meal). Place the cheese in a medium bowl.

6   In a medium heavy saucepan, heat the milk over medium-high heat until it is hot, but not boiling. Add the farina and cook for 2 minutes, stirring constantly, until the mixture is slightly thickened. Pour the farina over the cheese and stir to combine.

7   Pour the cheese mixture over the knafeh dough in the prepared pan, and smooth the top. Place in the oven and bake for 30-40 minutes, or until the knafeh is deep golden brown. Remove from the oven and cool for 15 minutes.

8   Turn the knafeh out onto a platter and drizzle with ¼ cup of orange blossom syrup. Garnish with pistachio nuts. Serve immediately or set aside and reheat before serving. Cut into squares or slices and serve the knafeh warm, with more orange blossom syrup poured over each piece.

Sour cream Rhubarb Crisp   Corry Wink

Ingredients

4 cups rhubarb or 3 cups rhubarb   1 cup sliced strawberries
1 1/2 cups granulated sugar   1/3 cup all purpose flour
1 cup sour cream (I use 14% sour cream)
1/3 cup soft butter   2/3 cup brown sugar
1/3 cup rolled oats   1/3 cup all purpose flour

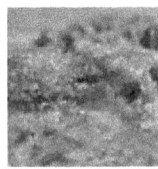

Sour cream Rhubarb Crisp[148]

Instructions

1. Arrange the rhubarb in a baking dish scatter the strawberries on top if using.
2. Mix sour cream and sugar and pour it evenly over the rhubarb.
3. Combine butter, brown sugar, rolled oats and flour and sprinkle on top of fruit.
4. Bake at 450 degrees for 15 min. Reduce temperature to 350 degrees and bake for an additional 30 minutes or until fruit is tender and crumbs are golden.
5. This can also be baked in a 10-inch pie crust.

---

[148] https://www.allrecipes.com/recipe/9600/sour-cream-rhubarb-squares/

Caramelized Apple Puree   Corry Wink

Ingredients

1 1/2 cups sliced apples (granny smith are best)
1 tbsp canola oil   ¼ cup onion sliced
1/3 cup cider vinegar   2 tbsp brown sugar
Salt

Caramelized Apple Puree[149]

Instructions

1. Caramelize onion in oil
2. When onions have brown caramel colour, add apple
3. Cook for about 30 minutes (slowly) until apples are caramelized.
4. Deglaze with water if the mixture sticks to the pot.
5. Add cider vinegar and brown sugar and cook for a few minutes more to reduce vinegar and to melt sugar.
6. Add salt to taste.
7. Puree the mixture in a blender.

---

[149]https://www.bing.com/search?q=Caramelized+Apple+%26+Pumpkin+Pie+Recipe

Recipes of Canadian Martyrs and St. Margaret Mary Church

Katie Coonen's Oreo Ice Cream Torte   Fr Tim Coonen

Ingredients

Mix 1 cup powdered sugar (mom's recipe calls for two cups!)
1/2 cup butter   1 can evaporated milk (354 ml
or 12 oz, ordinary, not sweetened)   2/3 cup chocolate chips
Gently boil 8 minutes; (I use a double boiler), cool.
Oreo cookies, about 36 cookies: (500 g pkg leaves some extra), crush.

Oreo Ice Cream Torte[150]

Instructions

1. Combine with 1/3 cup melted butter. Reserve 1 cup for topping.
2. Spread in a 9 x 13 pan.
3. 1/2-gallon (2 liters) vanilla ice cream, spread over cookie crust
4. Sprinkle 1 cup salted Spanish peanuts (I use more).
5. Spread cooled (but still liquid) chocolate mixture over ice cream and peanuts. (at this stage I stick it into the freezer to set it up a bit; trying to spread cool whip over the soft glop isn't easy...).
6. Spread a layer of Cool Whip over all (my sisters use whipped cream from a can)
7. Sprinkle the reserved cup of cookie crumb mix over the Cool Whip.
8. Cover with plastic wrap and freeze.
9. Let stand at room temp 20 minutes before serving.

One note: the bagged Oreo cookie crumbs for sale look like an easy option, but I haven't tried them. I think the sweet filling in the actual cookies contributes to the integrity of the crust, not to mention the taste!

---

[150] https://www.bing.com/search?q=Frozen+Oreo+Torte&filters=ufn%3a%22Frozen+Oreo+Torte

Recipes of Canadian Martyrs and St. Margaret Mary Church
Delicious Coffee Cake — Louise Blanchet-Smith

Ingredients

Cream together these ingredients:
¼ cup butter   ¾ cup white sugar
2 eggs   1 ½ cups flour
1 tsp baking powder   1 tsp baking soda
1 cup sour cream   1 tsp vanilla
Mix together these ingredients for filling:
½ cup brown sugar   ½ cup walnuts
1 tsp cinnamon

Delicious Coffee Cake[151]

Instructions

1. Pour half the batter in greased Bundt pan.
2. Top with nut mixture and add the rest of batter.
3. Bake at 350 degrees for 35 minutes.

Enjoy!

---

[151] ttps://www.bing.com/search?q=Coffee+Cake

Walnut Romesco — Anonymous
(From House & Home magazine, February 2018, page 88)

Ingredients

1 cup toasted walnut halves
½ tsp smoked paprika
½ cup olive oil
½ tsp kosher salt (optional)
1 garlic clove, coarsely chopped
1 tbsp tomato paste
2 tsp white vinegar
Freshly ground black pepper, to taste
3 whole roasted peppers, seeds removed (can use store-bought)
Note: ½ to 1 tsp turmeric powder (optional)

Walnut Romesco[152]

Instructions

1. In food processor, combine all the ingredients and whirl until chunky paste forms.
2. This sauce/dip is delicious with vegetables and crackers, is a nice spread for sandwiches and can be added to salad dressings. The addition of turmeric is my variation to the basic recipe.

Serves: 6
Preparation Time: 15 minutes

---

[152] https://www.bing.com/images/search?q=Walnut+Romesco

Tea Biscuits — Heather Duggan

Ingredients

2 cups flour
½ cup milk
1 tablespoon baking powder
1 tub regular spreadable cream cheese

Tea Biscuits[153]

Instructions

1. Sift flour and baking powder together. With two butter knives or pastry cutter, cut in cream cheese.
2. Add milk and mix. On lightly floured surface, roll out dough to ¾ inch thick.
3. Cut out circles with drinking glass.
4. Bake on ungreased cookie sheet at 425°F for 12-15 minutes.

Options: substitute flavoured cream cheese (pineapple, strawberry) for regular cream cheese. Add raisins, cranberries, lemon zest, herbs, onions, or garlic etc.

---

[153]https://www.bing.com/search?q=Basic+Tea+Biscuits&filters

Maple pie

Heather Duggan

Ingredients

3 eggs, lightly
½ cup quick cooking oats
½ cup evaporated milk
¼ cup butter or margarine, melted
1 tsp. vanilla or maple extract

1 cup packed brown sugar
½ cup walnuts (optional)
½ cup maple syrup
Pinch salt

Maple pie[154]

Instructions

1. Combine eggs, brown sugar, oats, walnuts, evaporated milk, maple syrup, butter, vanilla extract and salt in medium bowl.
2. Whisk together until well blended.
3. Pour filling into pie shell.
4. Bake in a preheated 350°F oven until set, 35-40 minutes.
5. Let cool, then chill before slicing.

---

[154] https://cooking.nytimes.com/recipes/1019782-salted-maple-pie

Dog Biscuits — Heather Duggan

Ingredients

2 ½ cups whole wheat flour
1 tsp sugar
1 tsp salt or bullion powder
1 egg

½ cup non-fat dry milk powder
¾ cup water
6 tbsp. vegetable oil

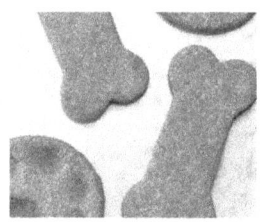

Dog Biscuits[155]

Instructions

1. Mix flour, milk powder, sugar, and salt together in medium bowl.
2. In a second bowl, mix oil, egg and water.
3. Mix with dry ingredients until it forms a ball.
4. Roll out ½ inch thickness on floured surface.
5. Cut into squares with knife or use a cookie cutter.
6. Place on greased baking sheet.
7. Bake at 350oF for 30 minutes.
8. Cool on rack.

---

[155] https://www.bing.com/search?q=Dog+Biscuits&filters=ufn%3a%22Dog+Biscuits

Chocolate Cherry Balls   Joseph Duggan

Ingredients

6 tbsp. Cocoa sifted
2 cups graham cracker crumbs
24 candied/glace cherries (approx.)
2 tbsp margarine
1 1/3 cup (1 tin) Eagle Brand milk

Chocolate Cherry Balls[156]

Instructions

1. Melt margarine in double boiler or heavy saucepan.
2. Add cocoa, then the Eagle Brand milk and cook gently until thickened.
3. Add graham cracker crumbs, cool slightly, mould around glace cherries and roll in chocolate wafer crumbs or chocolate.

---

[156] https://www.bing.com/search?q=Chocolate+Cherry+Balls&

Recipes of Canadian Martyrs and St. Margaret Mary Church

Overnight Buns   Duggan family

Ingredients

Mix in small bowl:
1 pkg. (2 ¼ tsp) yeast   ¼ cup warm water
1 tsp sugar   Let rise 10 minutes
Combine:
4 cups water   ¾ cup sugar
2 beaten eggs   1 cup oil
1 tbsp salt   12 cups flour
Add yeast mixture and mix well.

Overnight Buns[157]

Instructions

1. Set at 4pm. Punch down at 7pm. Put on greased pans at 10pm. Cover with tea towels and let rise overnight.
2. Bake in the morning at 325°F. Notes: Make sure yeast is dissolved.
3. Mix well. Make half a batch unless you want a lot of buns!

---

[157] https://www.bing.com/search?q=No+Knead+Overnight+Buns&

Lazy Gourmet Carrot Cake — Linda O'Mara

Ingredients:

4 eggs
1 ¼ cups oil
2 tsp baking soda
¼ tsp nutmeg
½ tsp salt
1 cup crushed pineapple (well drained)
½ cup chopped walnuts
Cream cheese icing
6oz cream cheese
2 cups icing sugar
½ tsp vanilla

2 cups sugar
2 cups flour
1 tbsp cinnamon
1/8 tsp cloves
2 cups grated carrots
1 tsp vanilla

¼ cup melted butter
1 tsp lemon juice

Lazy Gourmet Carrot Cake[158]

Instructions

1. Butter and flour large 13x9 inch pan. Preheat oven to 350°F. Beat eggs until frothy. Gradually add sugar and oil to eggs; beat until light. Sift together flour, baking soda, cinnamon, nutmeg, cloves, and salt; add to egg mixture. Combine carrots, pineapple, vanilla, and walnuts with egg mixture; mix thoroughly. Pour into prepared pan. Bake for 50 minutes to 1 hour.
2. Cream cheese icing: Beat the cream cheese until smooth. Stir the melted butter in slowly. Add the icing sugar, lemon juice and vanilla; beat until smooth.

---

[158] https://www.smartschoolhouse-content/uploads/2020/04/IMG_4798.jpg

Recipes of Canadian Martyrs and St. Margaret Mary Church
Easy Sugar Cookies — Pamela Dixon

Ingredients

2 ¾ cups all-purpose flour
½ tsp baking powder
1 ½ cups white sugar
1 tsp vanilla

1 tsp baking soda
1 cup butter, softened
1 egg

Easy Sugar Cookies[159]

Instructions

1. Preheat oven to 375 °F or 190 °C.
2. In a small bowl, stir together flour, baking soda and baking powder. Set aside
3. In a large bowl (or mixing bowl), cream together the butter and sugar until smooth.* Beat in the egg and vanilla. Gradually blend in the dry ingredients. Roll rounded teaspoonful of dough into balls, and placed onto ungreased cookie sheets (or cookie sheets with silpats or parchment paper). You could also use a teaspoon scoop to divide the dough into portions.
4. Bake 8 to 10 minutes in preheated oven, or until golden. Let stand on cookie sheet for a couple of minutes before removing to wire racks to finish cooling. *I whip the butter by itself for a few minutes before adding the sugar. The butter should change colour and become fluffy.

---

[159]https://www.bing.com/search?q=Easy+Sugar+Cookies&filters

Chocolate Chip Coffee Cake Easy Chocolate Cake

Marion Lochnan

Ingredients

Blend:
1 c. Melted butter
2 eggs
1 1/2 c. white sugar
1 cup Sour cream
2 tsp. Vanilla
2 T. Milk

Sift together:
2 cups All purpose flour
1 tsp. Baking sofa
1/2 to 3/4 c. Mini chocolate chips
1 ½ tsp. Baking Powder Potato scones

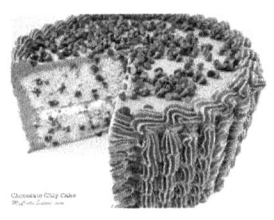

Chocolate chip Cake[160]

Instructions

1. Add dry ingredients to the butter mixture until blended.
2. Add mini chocolate chips. Grease and flour a Bundt pan.
3. Bake at 350 for 50 min. Cool for 10 min. Turn onto wire rack.
4. When cooled, dust with icing sugar if desired.

---

[160] https://www.bing.com/images/search?view=detailV2&ccid=fy%2beVQh9&id=4F6D77D7E6AAD33C70D913FB317C030F0BE5E7EE&thid=OIP.fy-eVQh9Rsk5Q_

Easy Chocolate Cake
Marion Lochnan

Ingredients

Sift:
2 cup White sugar
Baking powder
1 tsp. Salt
Add:
1 cup Milk
2 tsp. Vanilla

1 3/4 cup All purpose floor 1/2 tsp.
1 1/2 tsp. baking soda
3/4 c. Unsweetened cocoa

1/2 c. Vegetable oil

Easy Chocolate Cake[161]

Instructions

1. Mix for two minutes on medium speed.
2. Stir in 1 c. Boiling water. Batter is thin.
3. Pour into a greased and floured Bundt pan.
4. Bake 350 for 35-40 min. In preheated oven.
5. Bake for a few extra minutes if necessary.
6. When cooled, dust with icing sugar if desired.

---

[161] https://www.bing.com/search?q=Easy+Chocolate+Cake&filters=ufn%3a%2 2Easy+Chsocolate+Cake

Recipes of Canadian Martyrs and St. Margaret Mary Church

Potato Scones   Marion Lochnann

Ingredients

2 cup flour
3 tsp .baking powder
1 cup mashed potatoes

3/4 tsp. salt
cut in 3 tbsp. shortening

Potato Scones[162]

Instructions

1. Beat 1 egg and 1/2 c. Milk. Mix slowly with above ingredients. Add extra milk if needed. The mixture is quite dry.
2. Empty contents onto a floured surface.
3. Pat or roll into desired thickness (mine is usually 1/2 inch or slightly more). Use a glass to cut out the scones. Melt shortening in a pan and cook scones slowly on both sides. Butter melts instantly when spread on scones.

---

[162] https://www.bing.com/search?q=Gluten-Free+Sweet+Potato+Scones&

Best chocolate zucchini brownies — Nicole Lance

Ingredients

Brownies
2/3 cup vegetable oil
1/2 cup semi-sweet or dark chocolate chips
2 tablespoons unsweetened cocoa powder
1 cup granulated sugar (note: when doubling the recipe, still only use 1 cup sugar)
1 egg
1 tsp vanilla
1/4 tsp baking soda
1 egg yolk
1 cup all-purpose flour
1/2 tsp salt
1 cup grated zucchini - excess moisture squeezed out
Frosting
3 tbsp butter
1 1/2 tsp unsweetened cocoa powder
3 tbsp semi-sweet chocolate chips
1 1/2 tbsp milk
1 cup powdered sugar
1/4 tsp vanilla

Best chocolate zucchini brownies[163]

Instructions

1. Preheat oven to 350 degrees. Line a 9x9 baking pan with foil and lightly spray with non-stick cooking spray.
2. In a medium saucepan over medium low heat, combine oil, chocolate chips, and cocoa, whisking or stirring occasionally, until chips are melted, and mixture is smooth. Remove from heat and whisk in the

---

[163] https://www.bing.com/search?q=Chocolate+Zucchini+Brownies&filters=ufn%3a%22Chocolate+Zucchini+Brownies

sugar. Then add the eggs and vanilla, and whisk until combined. Stir in the zucchini. Fold in the flour, baking soda, and salt, until batter is well-combined, but do not over mix.
3. Spread batter into prepared pan and bake for 20-25 minutes, or until a toothpick inserted in the center comes out clean or with only a few moist crumbs.
4. While the brownies bake, melt together the butter, cocoa, chocolate chips, and milk in a small or medium saucepan over medium low or low heat. Remove from heat and whisk in the vanilla and powdered sugar, until combined and smooth.
5. When the brownies come out of the oven, pour the frosting on and spread it evenly over the top. Cool for 5-10 minutes, then lift foil to remove brownies from pan, cut into pieces, and serve.

Recipes of Canadian Martyrs and St. Margaret Mary Church

Crème Brule Cheesecake   Elinor Russell

Ingredients

Crust:
1 ¾ cup gingersnap crumbs   2 tbsp salt
¼ tsp salt   1/3 cup butter
500 ml. whipping cream

Crème Brule Cheesecake

Instructions

1. Preheat oven to 350°F. Prepare a 9 ½ inch spring form pan. Tear off an 18 inch square of heavy duty aluminum foil. Wrap the foil over edges of pan, crimping at top so it is secure.
2. Repeat with second and third sheet of foil. Combine four ingredients. Press into bottom of pan and bake for 10 minutes.

Cake:
Reduce oven to 325°F
3 pkgs (250 g.) cream cheese, room temperature
1 1/3 cup sugar
1 tsp vanilla
¼ tsp salt
1 ½ cups heavy cream
10 large egg yolk

1. Beat cream cheese for 4 minutes.
2. Add sugar, vanilla, salt and beat for another 4 minutes.
3. Heat cream in a small pot on low heat until it is warm but doesn't boil.
4. Beat egg yolks for 2 minutes until they are pale yellow. Pour heated cream through a fine mesh strainer into glass measuring cup
5. While mixer is going, slowly add warm cream. Eggs will curdle if you do not do this slowly.

Recipes of Canadian Martyrs and St. Margaret Mary Church

Chocolate Mounds Elinor Russell

Ingredients

8 squares semi-sweet Chocolate 1 tin eagle brand condensed milk
1 cup walnuts, pecans, or almonds ½ cup shredded coconut

Chocolate Mounds[164]

Instructions

1. Melt chocolate, add milk.
2. Cook in microwave for 2 minutes on high, stirring after 1 minute.
3. Add other ingredients, mix. (I added more nuts and coconut. You could also add Rice Krispies or oatmeal.)
4. Line cookie sheet with parchment paper. Drop by teaspoon on lined cookie sheet, refrigerate until set.

---

[164] https://www.kraftwhatscooking.ca/recipe/chocolate-mounds-127039

Cheesecake Cupcakes — Elinor Russell

Ingredients

24 paper muffin cups
1 cup sugar
1 pkg vanilla wafers (I have used other flat round cookies as well)
4 eggs
2 tsp lemon juice
3 9-oz packages of cream cheese, softened.
Cherry, blueberry, or raspberry pie filling

Cheesecake Cupcakes[165]

Instructions

1. Preheat oven to 350 degrees.
2. Mix sugar, cheese, eggs, and lemon juice until smooth. Line cupcake pans with papers.
3. Place one wafer in the bottom of each.
4. Spoon cheese mixture over wafers to fill cups 3/4 full. Bake in preheated oven for 18 to 20 minutes. Cool. Cupcakes will sink in the middle while cooling.
5. Spoon pie filling on each cupcake and refrigerate at least one hour. These may be topped with a whipped topping if desired. Serves 24.

---

[165] https://www.bing.com/search?q=Strawberry+Cheesecake+Cupcakes&filters

Whitewater Granola Bars   Elinor Russell

Ingredients

1 cup butter
1 ½ tsp vanilla
1 cup corn syrup
1 cup cocoanut toasted
1 cup sesame seeds, toasted
1 ½ cups peanut butter
2 cups brown sugar
6 cups rolled oats
1 cup sunflower seeds, toasted
2 cups chocolate chips, or 1 cup raisins & cup chocolate chips

Whitewater Granola Bars[166]

Instructions
1. In a skillet, toast cocoanut, sunflower seeds, and sesame seeds. Set aside to cool
2. In a large mixing bowl, cream together butter, peanut butter, vanilla, and brown sugar.
3. Add corn syrup and then mix in remaining ingredients. Press into greased 12 x 18 inch cookie sheet. Bake in a 350°F oven for approximately 20 minutes, or until golden brown. Let cool slightly and cut while still warm.
4. *substitute toasted almonds and I tsp almond extract for sunflower seeds and vanilla if you want to switch it up a little.

---

[166] https://i.pinimg.com/736x/75/b3/d4/75b3d4d25c70672b8c4dfdfc25b19f72.jpg

Recipes of Canadian Martyrs and St. Margaret Mary Church
Grandma Grady's Apple Pie   Rosemarie Hoey

Ingredients:

Pastry:
1 ½ cups of pastry flour   ½ tsp. white salt
½ cup of Tender Leaf shortening   Cold water to knead do
Filling:
4-5 large apples (McIntosh preferred)
1 cup of granulated sugar   ¼ tsp. cinnamon
1/8 tsp. nutmeg   1/8 tsp. salt
2 tsp. of pastry flour   1 tbsp. of lemon juice
1 tbsp. of melted butter

Grandma Grady's Apple Pie[167]

Instructions

Pastry:

1. Ensure that all ingredients are as cold as possible.
2. Sift dry ingredients into a large bowl.
3. Cut shortening into dry ingredients with pastry knife.
4. Using the knife, firmly mix in enough water to stiffen
5. the dough. Lightly dust the board and rolling pin.
6. Divide the dough in half. Roll one half to line a lightly
7. greased 9 in. pie plate. Prick shell for shaping and air.

Filling:

8. Quarter and cut peeled apples into 1/16 in. slices.

---

[167]https://i.pinimg.com/originals/67/4a/47/674a4771ddf2aa93c64327acc706be4d.jpg

Recipes of Canadian Martyrs and St. Margaret Mary Church

3. Place in heavy skillet. Add lemon juice.
4. Combine sugar, spices, salt, and flour. Stir into apples.
5. Cover skillet & steam over low heat until apples are soft.
6. Spoon hot apples into unbaked crust.
7. Drizzle melted butter over mixture.
8. Cover with top crust which has been slashed and/or
9. decorated with pastry cutouts to allow steam to escape.
9. Bake for 15-20 minutes in a hot 450°F oven.

The Grady Bakery was established in Peterborough, ON in the 1880s and retained a very special reputations for its crusty breads, pies, and sweets until its closure in the 1960s. Johanna Twomey Grady adjusted her father-in-law's recipe for multiple pies to a more manageable recipe for a single pie which could be readily adapted to a dozen ',kpie tarts' and use cookie cutters for a seasonal cap of a pumpkin, holly, or plain round shape for smaller appetites. This pie filing method can keep refrigerated for several days and can be varied by adding personal choices of a cup of dried fruit such as raisins or cranberries. As children, we preferred just the apples but served warm with Kawartha Diary ice cream or Empire Cheddar cheese. A Sunday treats!)

Cinnamon Swirl Apple Bread — Kelly Ann Beaton
Once Upon A Chef

Ingredients:

1/2 cup light brown sugar (packed)   1-1/2 tsp ground cinnamon
2 large eggs   1/2 cup gran lated sugar
1/2 cup (1 stick) unsalted butter, melted and slightly cooled
1/2 cup milk   2 tsp vanilla extract
1-1/2 c all-purpose flour, spooned into measuring cup and levelled off
1/2 tsp salt   1-1/2 tsp baking powder
1 cup peeled, cored, and finely diced tart baking apples, from 1 apple (preferably Granny Smith)

Cinnamon Swirl Apple Bread

Instructions

1. Preheat the oven to 350°F and set an oven rack in the middle position. Spray an 8.5 x 4.5-inch loaf pan lightly with non-stick cooking spray. Line the long side of the pan with a parchment paper "sling" and spray lightly with non-stick cooking spray again.
2. In a small bowl, mix the brown sugar and cinnamon until evenly combined. Set aside.
3. In the bowl of an electric mixer fitted with the paddle attachment or beaters, beat the eggs and granulated sugar on medium speed until pale and creamy, about 2 minutes.
4. With the mixer on low, gradually add the melted butter followed by the milk and vanilla and mix just until evenly combined.

Recipes of Canadian Martyrs and St. Margaret Mary Church

5. Add the flour, salt, and baking powder to the batter and mix on low speed until evenly combined.
6. Add the apples to the batter and fold with a rubber spatula until evenly incorporated.
7. Spoon about 2/3 of the batter into the prepared pan. Sprinkle about 2/3 of the brown sugar-cinnamon mixture on top of the batter. Spoon the remaining batter over top, followed by the remaining brown sugar-cinnamon mixture. Using a butter knife, swirl the layers by making a zig-zag motion through the batter once in each direction (don't overdo it!).
8. Bake for about 50 minutes, until the bread is golden brown, and a cake tester or toothpick inserted into the center comes out clean. Let the bread cool on a rack for about 30 minutes, then use the parchment sling to lift the bread out of the pan and onto the rack. Let cool completely before slicing, a few hours or overnight. Store loosely covered with aluminum foil on the countertop for up to 4 days.
9. A lovely apple bread with a generous cinnamon swirl and crisp sugared top. So so yummy
10. Servings: One 8.5 x 4.5 inch loaf

Prep Time: 30 Minutes
Time: 55 Minutes
Total Time: 1 Hour 25 Minutes

Apple Cake Tartin - Ina Garten — Kelly Ann Beaton
Cinnamon Swirl Apple Bread

Ingredients

6 tbsp (3/4 stick) unsalted butter, at room temperature, plus extra for greasing the dish 3/4 cups granulated sugar, divided
1 1/4 Granny Smith apples, peeled and sliced into 12 pieces
2 extra-large eggs, at room temperature 1/3 cup sour cream
1/2 tsp grated lemon zest 1/2 tsp pure vanilla extract
1 cup plus 2 tablespoons all-purpose flour 1/2 tsp baking powder
1/4 tsp kosher salt Confectioners' sugar

Apple Cake Tartin - Ina Garten

Instructions

1. Preheat the oven to 350°F.
2. Generously butter a 9-inch glass pie dish and arrange the apples in the dish, cut side down.
3. Combine 1 cup of the granulated sugar and 1/3 cup water in a small saucepan and cook over high heat until it turns a warm amber color, about 360 degrees F on a candy thermometer. Swirl the pan but don't stir. Pour evenly over the apple slices.
4. Meanwhile, cream the 6 tablespoons of butter and the remaining 3/4 cup of granulated sugar in the bowl of an electric mixer fitted with the paddle attachment, until light and fluffy. Lower the speed and beat in the eggs 1 at a time. Add the sour cream, zest, and vanilla and mix until combined. Sift together the flour, baking powder, and salt and, with the mixer on low speed, add it to the butter mixture. Mix only until combined.
5. Pour the cake batter evenly over the apple slices and bake for 30 to 40 minutes, until a cake tester comes out clean. Cool for 15 minutes, then invert the cake onto a flat plate. If an apple slice sticks, ease it

out and replace it in the design on top of the cake. Serve warm or at room temperature, dusted with confectioners' sugar.
6   This is another yummy weekend dessert for family and friends.

Hot Fudge Pudding — Angela Davis

Ingredients

1 cup flour
¼ tsp salt
½ cup butter melted
½ cup milk
1 ½ cup hot water

1 ½ cup sugar (divided)
1 tsp baking powder
½ cup cocoa (divided)
1 tsp vanilla
½ cup nuts (optional)

Hot Fudge Pudding

Instructions

1. Using a 9" baking dish add flour, ¾ c sugar and dry ingredients and mix. Melt butter with ¼ c cocoa. Add to dry ingredients with milk and vanilla, mix.
2. Combine ¾ c sugar and ¼ c cocoa and pour all over batter. Don't stir.
3. Bake at 350°F, 40- 45 minutes.
4. I have put the walnuts or pecans in the batter and in the sauce and it works out well. My family loves it. Not much to clean up.

Blueberry Kuchen   Kathy Armstrong

Ingredients

1 cup plus 2 tablespoons flour, divided   1/8 tsp salt
2 tbsp plus 2/3 cup sugar, divided   1 tbsp white vinegar
5 cups blueberries, divided   1/8 tsp cinnamon
½ cup butter, slightly softened (cold for food processor)

Blueberry Kuchen

Instructions

1. In a medium bowl, mix 1 cup flour, salt, and 2 tbsp sugar. Cut in butter until particles resemble coarse crumbs. Sprinkle with vinegar. Shape into dough and with lightly floured fingers press into loose-bottom 9-inch springform pan – about ¼ inch thick on bottom, less thick and 1 inch high around sides. Add 3 cups blueberries. Mix remaining 2 tbsp flour with remaining 2/3 cup sugar and the cinnamon. Sprinkle over blueberries.
2. Bake on lowest rack in preheated 400°F oven for 50-60 min (Check after 40 minutes if you use convection) or until crust is well browned and filling bubbles.
3. Remove from oven to rack. Sprinkle with remaining 2 cups blueberries. Cool. Remove rim of pan.

Boule de Neige   Kathy Armstrong

Ingredients

1 pint heavy cream, whipped
1 cup icing sugar
1 pint any other flavour sherbet
½ cup chopped walnuts
1 pint any flavour sherbet

Boule de Neige

Instructions

1. Combine whipped cream, nuts, and sugar. Line bowl with plastic wrap.
2. Line a 1 ½ quart bombe mold (stainless steel mixing bowl) with whipped cream mixture, leaving a hollow in the center.
3. Put in freezer while you stir sherbet to soften a bit. Fill hollow with sherbet – one colour at a time.
4. Cover with foil and freeze several hours…or days. When ready to serve, let sit at room temperature about 10 minutes.
5. Turn out on a fancy plate – take a bow!

Banana Bread (wheat free options)   McE Galbreath

Ingredients

3-4 ripe bananas   1 cup brown sugar
½ cup butter   2 eggs
2 cups of flour (spelt or brown rice work well)
Optional: ¼ cup semi-sweet chocolate chips
1 tsp baking soda

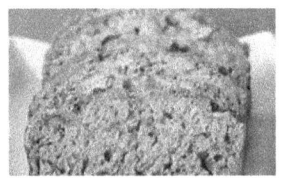

Banana Bread

Instructions

1. Preheat oven to 350°F. Grease a loaf pan.
2. Melt butter in the microwave, add in the sugar and eggs. Stir. Then add in the bananas (peeled and chopped) and stir all up until all the ingredients are thoroughly combined.
3. Add baking soda to the flour of your choice. Add flour mixture to the "wet" ingredients and mix thoroughly.
4. If you wish, you can add chocolate chips to your dough mixture.
5. Scoop banana bread mush into a loaf pan and put it in the oven to bake.
6. Bake at 350°F for 1 hour, checking it at 50 mins. Use a toothpick to determine doneness; insert the toothpick and pull it out. The loaf is ready when the toothpick comes out clean!

Yummy every time!

Flourless Chocolate Cake (GF) — McE Galbreath

Ingredients

2 cups almonds, ground
½ cup sweetened cocoa powder
1/3 cup unsweetened extract
½ tsp salt

1 cup packed brown sugar
1 tsp almond vegetable oil
4 large eggs, separated
Frosting or sugar drizzle

Flourless Chocolate Cake

Instructions

1. Preheat oven to 350°F. Grease round or square baking pan.
2. Grind almonds into a fine flour. Mix in brown sugar, oil and cocoa, almond extract, salt, and egg yolks.
3. Beat egg whites until stiff. Then fold them carefully into the chocolate/almond mixture.
4. When the mixture is well combined, scoop it into the baking pan.
5. Bake for 40-45 minutes and test with a toothpick for doneness.
6. Great with ice cream, or just on its own!!

Recipes of Canadian Martyrs and St. Margaret Mary Church

Poor Boy Cake — Patrick Zdunich

Ingredients

1¾ cups of water
½ cup of butter
1 cup sugar
1 tsp salt
1 tsp cinnamon
1 tsp allspice
½ cup icing sugar

1 cup of rinsed raisins.
2 cups flour
1 tsp baking soda
1 tsp cloves
1 tsp nutmeg
1 slightly beaten egg
2 tsp of lemon juice.

Poor Boy Cake

Instructions

1. Preheat oven to 375°F. Butter a 9 x 13 inch lasagne pan. (You can use a larger cookie sheet but reduce bake time by about 5 minutes)
2. Put 1¾ cups of water in a pot and add 1 cup of rinsed raisins. Boil for about 10 minutes to reduce liquid to 1 cup. Add water if required. Remove from heat.
3. Add ½ cup of butter to water and raisins and let the butter melt.
4. While the above is boiling, in a bowl mix: cups flour, 1 cup sugar, 1 teaspoon baking soda, 1 teaspoon salt, 1 teaspoon cloves (if you like spices, make all these rounded teaspoons), 1 teaspoon cinnamon, 1 teaspoon nutmeg, 1 teaspoon allspice; add to the dry ingredients, add 1 slightly beaten egg.
5. Add the liquid and raisins and stir gently. Pour into the buttered lasagne pan and cook for 23 minutes. Check for done using a toothpick in the centre.
6. While the cake is still warm, mix ½ cup icing sugar with 2 tsp of lemon juice. Drizzle evenly on the cake and spread gently with the back of a spoon. Cut into pieces, pour a cup of coffee, and enjoy!

Total time 40 minutes
. Whenever I make my mum's Poor Boy Cake for a Holy Canadian Martyrs event, I always get at least one request for the recipe. I hope this delicious spice cake from my childhood makes some good memories for you, too. It's also great for when you need to bring something somewhere in a real hurry.

Recipes of Canadian Martyrs and St. Margaret Mary Church

Aunt Julia's Torte   Fr. Tim Coonen

Ingredients

1 stick of margarine (1/2 cup)　　　　1 cup flour
1 cup walnuts, broken
Mix together:
8 oz. cream cheese (softened, room temp.)　1 cup powdered sugar
½ of a container of Cool Whip (recipe says 9 oz but I use 12oz)
Put on cooled crust

Aunt Julia's Torte

Instructions

1. Mix margarine and flour then add the nuts. Press into 9x13 pan and bake at 350°F for 15 minutes.
2. 3 cups milk, mixed with two 3 ¾ oz boxes of instant butterscotch pudding. (Mix per box instructions, spread on top next.
3. Then spread the rest of the Cool Whip on top.
4. Sprinkle something on top if you like: chopped nuts, with a dash of salt, or crushed candy like Skor bars, etc.
5. This need refrigeration.

This can be made with any flavour pudding. Chocolate with pecans instead of walnuts is good. Pistachio is good, and green in colour if you need that for St. Patrick's Day, for instance. Crushed Skor bars on top of that.

Plum (or other fruit) Custard "Pie" Terri White Lobsinger
(Source: The Ottawa Citizen, many years ago with adaptations by Terri)

Ingredient

1 2/3 cup flour
½ tsp salt, ½ tsp salt
½ cup (+2 tbsp) butter
2 beaten eggs

½ tsp. baking powder
2 ½ tbsp. sugar
½ tsp. cinnamon

Plum (or other fruit) Custard "Pie"

Instructions

1. Preheat oven to 400°F   Use a 9" square pan.
2. Mix together: 1 2/3 cup flour, ½ tsp. baking powder, ½ tsp salt, and   2 ½ tbsp. sugar
3. Cut in until crumbly: ½ Cup (+2 tbsp) butter. Pat mixture into bottom and up the sides of the pan.
4. Arrange nicely over the pastry a variety of fruit: anything from 4-6 large black plums quartered with peel; or a mixture of strawberries (halved if large) and cut up rhubarb; or strawberries alone; or other fruit like peaches (with peel).
5. The next steps are good for all fruit.
6. Mix together ½ cup sugar and ½ tsp. cinnamon and sprinkle over fruit.
7. Bake for 15 minutes.
8. When the fruit base is baking, mix together: 2 beaten eggs, 1/2 cup sour cream (+ a bit more if desired), and ½ cup buttermilk, sour milk or yogurt.
9. After the bottom has baked for 15 minutes, remove the pan from the oven and drizzle the egg, 'cream' mixture over the heated-up fruit.

Recipes of Canadian Martyrs and St. Margaret Mary Church

    Return the pan to the oven and bake an additional 30 minutes. Serve warm or cold.
ENJOY because it is super delicious!
Note: it is fine to freeze as well. (Reheat frozen pie in a 325°F oven for 45-60 minutes with a piece of foil wrap placed lightly on top.

A dessert that will serve 9 people but really won't because everyone will want a 2nd serving!!!

Recipes of Canadian Martyrs and St. Margaret Mary Church

Happiness Cake — Mary Hill

Ingredient

1 cup of good thoughts
2 cups well-beaten faults
2 cups forgiveness
1 cup consideration for others
1 cup kind deeds

Happiness Cake

Instructions

1. Mix thoroughly. Add tears of joy, sorrow and sympathy. Flavour with love and kindly service.
2. Fold in 4 cups of prayer and faith. Blend well. Fold into daily life.
3. Bake well with warmth and human kindness, and serve with a smile anytime. Make daily throughout the year.

Recipes of Canadian Martyrs and St. Margaret Mary Church
Blueberry Muffins   Kay Cedar

Ingredient

¼ cup butter
2 cups flour
½ tsp salt
½ cup milk
2 cups blueberries

1 ¼ cups sugar
2 eggs
2 tsp baking powder
2 tsp sugar for top

Blueberry Muffins

Instructions

1. On low speed cream butter and sugar, add eggs one at a time, and blend sifted ingredients.
2. Add milk then slowly fold in the blueberries. Fill well-greased muffin pans, and sprinkle sugar on top. Lightly grease tops as they bake.
3. Bake at 375 F for app. 25 minutes. Yields one dozen large muffins.

Almond Biscotti Gina Downing

Ingredient

1 ¾ cup flour
¾ cup unblanched almonds
2 eggs
⅓ cup melted butter
1 tsp grated orange rind

2 tsp baking powder
¾ cup sugar
2 tsp vanilla extract
½ tsp almond extract
1 egg white lightly beaten

Almond Biscotti

Instructions

1. Combine flour, baking powder and almonds. Beat together eggs, sugar, butter, vanilla, almond extract and orange rind. Divide dough in half and form 2-10 inch long logs. Brush logs with egg white and place on un-greased cookie sheet.
2. Bake at 350 F for 20 minutes. Remove from oven and let cool for 5 minutes. Transfer logs to cutting board and cut diagonally into slices 3/4 inch thick. Stand cookies upright on cookie sheet and bake another 25 minutes. Remove from oven and let cool. 4 servings

Recipes of Canadian Martyrs and St. Margaret Mary Church
Double Chocolate Brownies — Gina Downing

Ingredient

¾ cup flour
¾ cup sugar
2 cups semi-sweet chocolate chips, divided
⅓ cup butter
½ cup chopped nuts
¼ tsp salt
2 eggs
¼ tsp baking soda
2 tbsp. water
1 tsp. vanilla extract

Double Chocolate Brownies

Instructions

1. Preheat oven to 325 F. In a small bowl, combine flour, baking soda and salt. Set aside. In small saucepan, combine butter, sugar and water. Bring to a boil, then remove from heat.
2. Add 6 oz. (1 cup) chocolate chips and vanilla. Stir till chips melt and mixture is smooth. Transfer to a large bowl.
3. Add eggs, one at a time, beating well after each addition. Gradually blend in flour mixture. Stir in the remaining cup of chips, and the nuts.
4. Spread into a 9 inch square baking pan. Bake 30 to 35 minutes. Cool completely cut into squares. Makes 16 x 1/4 inch squares. 8 servings

Oatmeal Lace Cookies
Gina Downing

Ingredient

2 cups Quaker oats
1 egg
½ cup flour
½ cup butter

1 tsp. baking powder
2 cups brown sugar, well packed
pinch salt

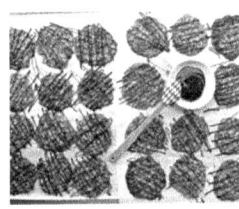

Oatmeal Lace Cookies

Instructions

1 Mix all dry ingredients together.
2 Add beaten egg and melted butter.
3 Drop in small spoonfuls on an un-greased cookie sheet. Press down with a fork dipped in cold water.
4 Bake at 350 F for 10 minutes. Watch closely. Leave on cookie sheet to cool for 2 minutes after removing from oven.

Peanut Butter Marshmallow Treats   Gina Downing

Ingredients

2 small pkg. Butterscotch chips
1 cup peanut butter
1 cup coconut
½ cup butter
1 cup crushed peanuts

Peanut Butter Marshmallow Treats

Instructions

1. Melt chips and butter in double boiler over low heat.
2. Add to this mixture butter, peanuts and coconuts.
3. Add one bag miniature marshmallows (coloured). Mix well. Pour into a 9" x 13" pan and refrigerate.
4. When cool cut into squares.

Almond Butter Crunch
Gina Downing

Ingredients

1 ¼ white or brown sugar
1 cup butter (not margarine)
1 cup sliced or slivered almonds
6 oz. chocolate chips

1 tbsp. corn syrup
3 tbsp. water
1 cup sliced or slivered almonds
almonds for sprinkling

Almond Butter Crunch

Instructions

1 Boil to hard crack stage 310 F the butter, sugar, syrup and water. (Use candy thermometer).
2 Remove from heat, add almonds & stir. Pour onto cookie sheet.
3 Work quickly. Melt chocolate chips & spread over candy. Sprinkle with extra almonds.
4 Refrigerate until very cold. Break into pieces

Recipes of Canadian Martyrs and St. Margaret Mary Church

Chocolate Chip Cake — Danielle Manseau O'Byrne

Ingredients

1 cup of chopped dates
1 ½ tsp of baking soda
1 cup of sugar
1 1/3 cup of flower
¾ tsp of baking soda
1 cup chocolate chips

1 ½ cup of boiling water
¾ cup of shortening
2 eggs
¾ tsp of baking soda
¼ sugar
½ cup chopped nuts

Chocolate Chip Cake

Instructions

1. Combine chopped dates, boiling water and 1½ tsp baking soda and cool for 1 hour.
2. Adding one ingredient at a time, beat at high speed shortening, sugar and eggs.
3. Mix flower, ¾ tsp baking soda and salt, and add to the shortening mixture and date mixture.
4. Pour into a flat greased layer pan and add chocolate chips, ¼ sugar and ½ cup chopped nuts. Bake at 275 C for 30 to 35 minutes

Recipes of Canadian Martyrs and St. Margaret Mary Church

Hazelnut Vanilla Shortbread   Louise Rickenbacker

Ingredients

Ingredients

⅓ cup hazelnuts
⅓ cup icing sugar
pinch salt
¾ tsp vanilla

½ cup all-purpose flour
⅓ cup cornstarch
½ cup butter, softened

Hazelnut Vanilla Shortbread

Instructions

1. On baking sheet, toast hazelnuts in 350 F oven for 8 to 10 minutes or until darkened and fragrant. Transfer to clean tea towel; rub nuts vigorously to remove most of the skins.
2. Transfer nuts to food processor or mini-chopper; grind with 1 tbsp each of the flour and icing sugar until finely ground with a few larger pieces. In bowl, stir together hazelnut mixture, cornstarch, salt and remaining flour.
3. In large bowl, beat together butter, vanilla and remaining icing sugar until fluffy. Adding hazelnut mixture in 2 additions, stir to form soft dough. Press into 1/2 inch thick disc; wrap in plastic wrap and refrigerate for about 30 minutes or until firm.
4. On lightly floured surface, roll out disc to slightly more than 1/8 inch thickness. With cookie cutter, cut out cookies and transfer to ungreased baking sheet. Bake, 1 sheet at a time, in centre of 300 degree oven for 10 to 12 minutes or just until shortbread are firm. Let cool on pan on rack. Makes about 30 cookies.

Recipes of Canadian Martyrs and St. Margaret Mary Church

Rum Cake
Elizabeth Thorn

Ingredients

1 cup chopped pecans
1 yellow cake mix
1 105 g Jell O Vanilla instant pudding and pie filling
½ cup amber rum

4 eggs
½ cup water
½ cup cooking oil

Rum Cake

Instructions

1 Preheat oven to 325 F. Grease and flour bundt pan. Sprinkle nuts over bottom of pan.
2 Mix all cake ingredients together.
3 Pour batter over nuts. Bake 1 hour. Cool.
4 Invert on serving plate. Prick top. Drizzle and smooth glaze evenly over top and sides.
5 Allow cake to absorb glaze. Repeat till glaze is used up.

Glaze

½ cup butter
1 cup sugar

¼ water
½ cup rum

1 Melt butter in saucepan.
2 Stir in water and sugar.
3 Boil 5 minutes, stiffing constantly.
4 Remove from heat. Stir in rum. Optional: Decorate with border of sugar frosting or whipped cream.

Brandy Sauce
Olive Laforce

Ingredients

¼ cup butter
2 tbsp brandy
2 egg whites

1 cup icing sugar
2 egg yolks
¼ cup cream or mild

Brandy Sauce

Instructions

1. Cream butter; gradually add sugar, brandy, egg yolks, cream or milk.
2. Cook in double boiler until thick. Cool.
3. Beat egg whites until stiff, then add to first mixture. Store in refrigerator.
4. This is good over Christmas pudding

Recipes of Canadian Martyrs and St. Margaret Mary Church

Chocolate Peanut Butter Balls   Samantha Wilson

Ingredients

1 cup of peanut butter
1 ½ cups of powdered sugar
1 cup of chocolate chips

2 cups of rice krispies
¼ tsp of vanilla

Chocolate Peanut Butter Balls

Instructions

1. Over low heat melt the chocolate chips and set aside. In a medium bowl combine all other ingredients.
2. Blend well until mixture forms a dough-like substance. Roll into 1 inch balls. Using a toothpick or fork dip the balls into the chocolate until well coated.
3. Place onto a cookie sheet lined with wax paper. Refrigerate for at least 30 minutes.

Cranberry Bread

Anne Louise Mahoney

Ingredients

- 2 cups all-purpose flour
- 1 tbsp. of baking powder
- ⅔ cup orange juice
- 3 tbsp. margarine or butter, melted
- 1 ¼ cups whole cranberries
- ½ cup granulated sugar
- ½ tsp salt
- 2 eggs, beaten slightly
- ½ cup chopped walnuts
- 2 tsp grated orange rind

Cranberry Bread

Instructions

1. Preheat oven to 350 F. Grease an 8" x 4½" x 3" loaf pan. Sift flour, sugar, baking powder and salt into a mixing bowl.
2. Make a well in the middle of the sifted mixture and pour in the orange juice, eggs and melted margarine. Mix well without over-mixing.
3. Fold in walnuts, cranberries and orange rind. Pour batter into greased loaf pan and set on middle rack of the oven. Bake for 45 to 50 minutes or until a knife inserted in the centre comes out clean. Cool in pan for 10 minutes, then cool completely on rack.

Fiesta Cheese Dip Cake — Vania Gomez

Ingredients

1 cup ground blue tortilla chips
2 tbsp butter, melted
3 eggs
2 tsp chili powder
1 tsp. dried oregano
¼ tsp hot pepper sauce
3 tbsp all-purpose flour
2 pkg.250 g cream cheese
3 1 tbsp. lime juice
1 ½ tsp. ground cumin
¼ tsp salt
2 cups sour cream

Fiesta Cheese Dip Cake

Instructions

1. Combine ground tortilla chips, flour and butter; pat into bottom of greased 9-inch spring-form pan.
2. Center pan on large foil square; press up tightly to side of pan. Bake in 350 F oven for 10 minutes. Remove from oven and set aside. Reduce oven temperature to 325 F In a large bowl, beat cream cheese until softened; beat in eggs well, one at a time.
3. Beat in lime juice chili powder, cumin, oregano, salt and hot pepper sauce; blend in sour cream. Pour onto base. Set pan into larger pan; pour in enough hot water to come an inch up side.
4. Bake for about 35 minutes or until edge is set but center still jiggles slightly. Quickly run knife around inside of pan. Turn oven off; let cool in oven for 1 hour. Remove pan from larger pan and remove foil; let cool on rack to room temperature. Cover and refrigerate for at least 8 hours or untill well chilled. (This can be refrigerated for up to 2 days) When ready to serve let stand at room temperature for 30 minutes. Transfer to serving platter.

Chocolate Peanut Butter Cake — Chris Rupar

Ingredients

1-cup graham crumbs
¼ cup butter, melted
12 oz cream cheese (1 ½ packages)
1 cup whipping cream – whipped
½ cup whipping cream (not whipped)
4 oz (4 squares) semisweet chocolate

¼ cup sugar
1 cup sugar
1 ½ cups peanut butter
1 ½ cup sugar
1 tsp vanilla
4 tbsp butter

Chocolate Peanut Butter Cake

Instructions

1. Combine graham crumbs, butter and sugar in a 9 inch spring foam pan and bake at 350F for 10 minutes.
2. Combine filling of cream cheese, peanut butter and sugar.
3. Add whipping cream and pour over crust.
4. Combine topping ingredients into sauce pan and stir medium-high to boil. Simmer for 5 minutes and remove from heat.
5. Add to mixture chocolate and butter and stir until chocolate melts, about 5 minutes. Pour over filling and refrigerate for 8 hours.
6.

Moist Shortcake
Danielle Le Banne

Ingredients

4 cups flour
1 tsp soda
1 tsp salt
2 cups sour milk

1 ½ tbsp baking powder
1 cup sugar
1 cup shortening

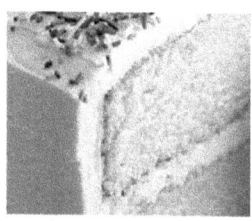

Moist Shortcake

Instructions

1. Cut shortening into dry ingredient and then add the milk.
2. Cook in a greased 9"x13" pan at 400F for about 20 minutes or until done.
3. You can sprinkle the top of the cake with sugar prior to baking. Serve with whipped cream, fresh strawberries or other fruit.

Julie's fluffy Frosting

Carol Lovejoy

Ingredients

1 egg white
½ cup butter or margarine
1 (6 oz.) can evaporated milk

1 cup sugar
2 heaping tbsp. Crisco

Julie's Fluffy Frosting

Instructions

1. Beat egg white until stiff. Beat sugar, butter and Crisco until smooth.
2. Fold in beaten egg white.
3. Heat evaporated milk to scalding (don't boil).
4. Slowly add (1 Tbsp. at a time) while beating.
5. Frosting will be very soft, but frosts beautifully and never gets hard.

Rhubarb Meringue Pie

Elizabeth Thorn

Ingredients

4 beaten egg yolks
3 tbsp. flour
⅛ tsp. salt
2-3 tbsp. Grand Marnier
rind of almost a whole large orange

1 cup sugar
2 tbsp. butter
3 tsp orange juice
4 cups diced rhubarb

Rhubarb Meringue Pie

Instructions

1. Combine together egg yolks, sugar, flour, butter and salt.
2. Add in rhubarb, orange rind, orange juice and Grand Marnier. Mix well.
3. Pour into unbaked shell and bake at 375 F for 35-45 minutes until set and lightly browned. Cool.
4. Top with meringue made with the 4 whites, bake fast at 400. You may wish to add a bit of orange peel to meringue before baking. Cool.

Sugar Pie   Mme Bertrand

Ingredients

2 cups light brown sugar
pinch of salt
1 tsp of butter
½ cup of milk

2 tsp of flour
¼ cup of corn syrup
½ cup of cream (35%)

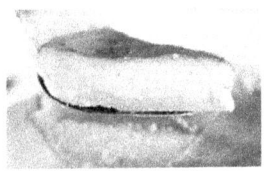

Sugar Pie

Instructions

1. Mix all ingredients. Cook for about 10 minutes in a pan on low heat. Use a pan with a thick bottom.
2. Let mixture mildly cool.
3. Pour on to your own pie crust.

Turtles
Alyson Farrell

Ingredients

25 wrapped caramels
1 cup of unsalted peanuts
2 tbsp of water

1 can chow mein noodles
3 tbsp butter
½ bag chocolate chips

Turtles

Instructions

1. Melt caramels in saucepan with butter and water. Fold in peanuts and noodles.
2. Drop bite size portions on wax paper or cookie sheet.
3. Melt chocolate chips with a tiny bit of water (2 tsp) on stove.
4. Drip over turtles.

Cherry Almond Nanaimo Bars. Anne Pehelman

Ingredients

½ cup margarine
⅓ cup cocoa
1 egg beaten
1 ¾ cup graham cracker crumbs
¼ cup butter softened
2 tbsp. maraschino cherry juice
⅓ cup chopped maraschino cherries
2 squares semi-sweet chocolate

¼ cup white sugar
1 tsp. vanilla
1 cup coconut
½ cup chopped almonds
1 tsp almond extract
2 cups icing sugar
1 tbsp butter

Cherry Almond Nanaimo Bars

Instructions

1. Bottom layer
2. Melt margarine, sugar and cocoa in pot over low heat. Remove from stove and add remaining ingredients. Pat firmly into a greased 9 inch square cake pan. Refrigerate 1 hour.
   Filling
3. Cream together butter, cherry juice and almond extract. Gradually beat in icing sugar until mixture is smooth and spreadable. Stir in chopped cherries and spread over bottom layer. Refrigerate until firm.
   Top layer
4. Heat chocolate and butter in double boiler or small saucepan over low heat, stirring until melted. Drizzle chocolate over filling. Chill.

Cheese Pie — Barb Popel

Ingredients

¼ cup melted butter
2 eggs
1 ¼ cup flour
½ tsp salt
½ lb cottage cheese
1 tsp sugar

¼ cup sugar
¾ cup milk
1 tsp baking powder
½ lb low fat cream cheese
1 egg
2 tbsp melted butter

Cheese Pie

Instructions

1. Mix batter of ¼ cup melted butter, sugar, eggs, flour, baking powder and salt.
2. Pour half in greased 9 inch square or round pan.
3. Mix filling of cream cheese, cottage cheese, 1 egg, sugar and 2 tbsp melted butter and spoon over batter.
4. Top with rest of batter. Bake at 350 F for 1 hour. Serve hot or store in refrigerator or freezer & reheat to serve.

Peanut Butter Bars Terry Murray

Ingredients

½ cup white sugar
1 cup peanut butter
2 cups rice krispies
1 tsp vanilla

½ cup corn syrup
½ cup crushed peanuts
1 cup corn flakes

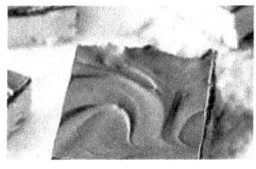

Peanut Butter Bars

Instructions

1. Melt sugar and corn syrup in top of double boiler (or try the microwave - heating about 2 min on Hi, stirring frequently).
2. In large bowl mix remaining ingredients (use two forks or your hands), then pour corn syrup mixture over and mix well, until all cereals are well coated.
3. Pack into lightly greased 8x8 inch pan; cut and serve.
4. Try spreading a thin layer of melted chocolate over top.
5. Melt 3 squares semi-sweet chocolate on Hi for 2-3 minutes and stir well.

Baked Apple Delight

Janet Bax

Ingredients

6 cups crisp, tart apples
1 ½ cups of plain yoghurt
lemon juice
sugar to taste

6 eggs
1 or 2 grated peel of lemons
2 tsp vanilla
2 tsp cinnamon

Baked Apple Delight

Instructions

1. Core and slice the apples (peeled optional) and place them in the glass casserole (butter lightly before filling)
2. Grate lemon peel over apples and then sprinkle cinnamon evenly over top.
3. Mix all other ingredients. Sprinkle with sugar. Pour mixture over apples.
4. Place in oven at 325 F for one hour.

Rhubarb-Orange Coffee Cake — Molly Fraser

Ingredients

Topping:
¼ cup brown sugar
½ tsp. cinnamon

Cake:
2 cups all purpose flour
2 tsp. baking powder
½ tsp. salt
1 tsp. vanilla
1 cup orange juice

1 tbsp. finely grated orange peel

¾ cup granulated sugar
½ tsp. baking soda
1 egg
⅓ cup melted butter
2 cups rhubarb, chopped

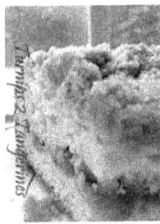

Rhubarb Orange Coffee Cake

Instructions

1 Preheat oven to 350 F. Grease 8 inch square pan.
2 Combine topping ingredients in a small bowl and set aside. Stir dry ingredients for cake together in a large bowl. In a smaller bowl, lightly beat egg; blend vanilla, butter and orange juice.
3 Pour egg mixture into dry mixture and stir until evenly combined. Do not over mix.
4 Spread half the batter into prepared pan. Cover evenly with rhubarb. Spoon remaining batter over top and spread gently.
5 Sprinkle topping mixture evenly over cake. Bake approximately 40 minutes, or until toothpick inserted into the centre comes out clean.
6 Serve warm or cool. Freezes well.

Recipes of Canadian Martyrs and St. Margaret Mary Church

Enjoy

www.ingramcontent.com/pod-product-compliance
Lightning Source LLC
Chambersburg PA
CBHW050105170426
43198CB00014B/2461